Praise for *Pow! Right Between the Eyes!*

"Great comedians call it 'the punch line,' where reality is shattered with brilliance and wit. When the punch line comes to marketing, Andy Nulman calls it a surprise—and he's a master at it. Read this book, and harness the power of *Pow!* in your business life."

—*Tim Sanders*, author, *The Likeability Factor*

"Well worth reading. *Pow!* is a fun and practical book with a wealth of stories and examples to definitely put you in a 'surprise someone' mindset. For example, when Andy shows us his 'balls,' it is done in a surprisingly tasteful way."

—*Roger von Oech*, author, *A Whack on the Side of the Head*

"I've always said: Be interesting, or be invisible. Andy teaches you how to start great word of mouth by surprising, delighting, and inspiring people to talk. You need this book!"

—*Andy Sernovitz*, author, *Word of Mouth Marketing: How Smart Companies Get People Talking*

"This book shows how to use the element of surprise to seize people's attention and shake up conventional mindsets, indispensable steps for anyone who wants to change the way they do business . . . or change the world."

—*David Bornstein*, author, *How To Change The World*

"In 30 years of coaching the best performers in the world, I found few that used both sides of their brain. Andy Nulman does! Now his rare, unique, and outrageous insights in *Pow!* will give you an edge over the competition."

—*Jim Fannin*, "Change Your Life" coach; author, *The S.C.O.R.E. System*

"Learning to implement surprise into your business model will not only influence your bottom line, but it will also have a profound side effect on your customers by opening the door to wonder, joy, and glee. Andy Nulman shows you how to do this and more in *Pow! Right Between the Eyes!*"

—*Loretta LaRoche,* author, speaker, and PBS star

"Thoroughly fun to read, Andy Nulman's *Pow!* surgically implants the concept of strategic surprise into your mind like a ticking time-bomb. Before you know it, you'll be layering surprises into your work all the time. For people whose earning power can be enhanced by bringing sudden delight to others, this book is a must. This includes anyone in business, design or marketing . . . and ambitious strippers."

—*Len Blum,* screenwriter, "Private Parts," "The Pink Panther," and yoga instructor

"The message you'll get within these pages: doing things in business that surprise and delight consumers creates a multitude of chain reactions that keep them engaged, entertained, thinking, talking about you and—most importantly—buying. *Pow! Right Between the Eyes* shows you how to ride the wave of sheer terror . . . and get a suntan. Make no mistake about it, adding surprise into your marketing mix isn't a shtick or stunt, it's a business imperative in this highly saturated media landscape."

—*Mitch Joel,* president, Twist Image and author of *Six Pixels of Separation*

POW!
RIGHT BETWEEN THE EYES!
PROFITING FROM THE POWER OF SURPRISE

Andy Nulman

**Original Illustrations by
Tim Barnard**

WILEY

John Wiley & Sons, Inc.

Published by John Wiley & Sons, Inc., Hoboken, New Jersey
Published simultaneously in Canada

For general information on our other products and services or for technical support, please contact our Customer Care Department within the United States at (800) 762-2974, outside the United States at (317) 572-3993 or fax (317) 572-4002.

Wiley also publishes its books in a variety of electronic formats. Some content that appears in print may not be available in electronic books. For more information about Wiley products, visit our web site at www.wiley.com.

Library of Congress Cataloging-in-Publication Data:

Nulman, Andy.
  Pow! right between the eyes: profiting from the power of surprise / Andy Nulman.
      p. cm.
  Includes index.
  ISBN 978-0-470-40550-5 (cloth)
  1. Marketing. I. Title.
  HF5415.N82 2009
  658.8—dc22
                                                                    2008036335

Printed in the United States of America

10 9 8 7 6 5 4 3 2 1

For Fitzy and The Sweet,
but especially for Ski

Pow!
Contents

Acknowledgments

Here's How a Book Is Born

In July 2006, marketing maven Mitch Joel asked me if I would be interested in presenting a case study at an event called CaseCamp. Instead of the standard, traditional case study model of "listen to what I've done," the one I would agree to present would be more like "listen to what I want to do," and focus on this curious theory that had been kicking around the back of my mind for about five years. So once again going against the grain, I presented a case for the power of Surprise, particularly in marketing. I swear on my life these were my blustery introductory words on that fateful day:

> *"Yes, I am presenting a case study ... but it's a case study about a book that has not yet been written. And I am the client. Actually, it's about more than a mere book. It's about a concept that could change the face of consumer marketing as we now know it. A concept that—if accepted—could change my entire career. Otherwise, why spend the time writing it?"*

Reaction to the concept that day was upbeat and positive, so after spending the summer researching the subject, I launched my "Pow! Right Between the Eyes!" blog in October to take it many steps further.

Over the Christmas holidays that year, I read, and was enamored with, Andy Sernovitz's book *Word of Mouth Marketing: How Smart Companies Get People Talking*, and said so a few times in the aforementioned blog. Sernovitz reached out to me by email to say thanks, I returned the reach via phone, and we became fast friends.

A little over a year later, in late January of 2008, we two Andys finally met face-to-face at the Shop.org conference in Orlando, where we were both keynoting. Over a late afternoon coffee, he mentioned that "Pow!" really should become a book, and gave me the names of two agents to contact to help make it so.

I called both upon my return home. One, the amazing Bill Gladstone of Waterside Productions, called back within five minutes; the other . . . well, I'm still waiting. After my spirited, "express-elevator pitch," Bill enthused, "I can sell this book!" and passed me over to his colleague Ming Russell, whose job it was to get me in shape to do so. Over the next month, Ming put me through a Pow!-prep boot camp, a torturous process that made the actual writing of this volume a cakewalk in comparison. On Friday, April 11, a mere 10 weeks after we first spoke, Bill lived up to his initial, excited words and confirmed the news as I walked off the stage from a speech to Wal-Mart: John Wiley & Sons, Inc., publisher had agreed to pick up the book. Pow! indeed.

Wiley's editorial tag-team of Shannon Vargo and Jessica Langan-Peck maintained the frenetic pace by requesting a final manuscript by August 1. Goodbye nights and weekends, hello SpellCheck! Their belief in (and boundless enthusiasm for) the project made the double-time tempo worthwhile. Together, we shared countless emails and voicemails, frantic phone calls where I tried to fit too many words into too few minutes, and live face-to-face visits where I met, and tried not to overwhelm, other dedicated Wiley-ites like Matt Holt, Christine Kim, Peter Knapp, Lauren Freestone, and Beth Zipko.

So cradle the volume you hold in your hands with tenderness and care; a lot of hard work and great people made it possible. Without them, I am nothing. And without the following folks, I'm even less, so thunderous thanks also go out to:

—My loving and supportive family, most notably my wife Lynn and my sons Aidan Foster and Hayes Brody, my dad Norman and late mom Carol, as well as Nancy and Steven Krychman, Stuart Nulman, Faigie Stark, and Seymour Coviensky, Howard and Joanne Harris, Gail and Henry Baragar, Barry Kirstein and Nicole Bertrand, Ali Kirstein, Hailey and Greggy Krychman, Justin and Laura Harris, and of course, my dogs Shaydee and Rawqui. Special props to Aidan for helping me research some of the more thorny parts of this book (but I'm still waiting for the Rabbis . . .).

—Brilliant business partners and faithful friends like Garner Bornstein, Gilbert Rozon, Bruce Hills, and Dean MacDonald.

—Tim Barnard, whose counterculture eye-popping marking-up of walls, comic books, t-shirts, snowboards, and sneakers made him the ideal visual accompaniment for this book.

—Mark Fortier, who goes way beyond the title and responsibilities of the term "publicist," my longtime National Speakers Bureau (NSB) speaking agents Theresa Beenken and Perry Goldsmith, who stuck with me through the toughest of hell gigs, and my newest speaking agent, he of much hard and great advice, Tom Neilssen of the BrightSight Group.

—The thousands of FOPs (Friends of Pow!) who have supported me and the power of Surprise via my blog posts and Twitter tweets.

—Scott Brooks, whose "you can never be too over-the-top" designs for my blog suddenly found themselves inspiring this book's front cover. Add to this his collaboration on all my videos and you know why Brooksie is Pow!'s unsung artistic MVP.

—Other creative collaborators like CommerceTel's Dennis Becker and Chris McGibbon; Wave Generation's Mike Elman; pop artist Steve Kaufman and his manager Barry Steinberg; the smartest man in the world, Saul Colt; and my faithful assistant, Nancy Essebag.

—The artists and musicians and authors that color my imagination and inflate my soul.

—Business-book writers like Tom Peters, Roger von Oech, Tim Sanders, Seth Godin, Al Ries, Jack Trout, Malcolm Gladwell, Jim Collins, Dan Pink, Douglas Rushkoff, Chip Heath, and Dan Heath, whom I have long admired and have tried hard to live up to within these pages.

—The fashion designers who continually provide the packaging, particularly Sal and Rosie Parasuco, Ida Mirijello and Linda DelPercio at Parasuco; Dig P.R.'s Susanne Weinberg and Strellson's Mark Altow; and of course, the Marcs—Marc Fernandez and Marc Ecko himself at Ecko Unltd.

—The spirit of creativity, that sprite that somehow always manages to find me when I am in need of it most.

—Finally, and most importantly: You. Together, we are a team.

So let me close this off with the exact same words I prophetically used to close off that fabled case study way back when:

"Surprise! I'm done . . .

. . . or perhaps, I'm just getting started."

And now, on with the show!

The Value of Surprise

John Cleese is one of the founding members of the legendary Monty Python's Flying Circus *and is modestly renowned as a God in the comedy, film, and television worlds.*

Throughout my lengthy and illustrious career, from the beginning of Monty Python to the collapse of the communist system, I have learned the importance and value of surprise.

I once went to bed with the Duke of Kent.

There! You see what I mean? You were surprised by learning that I had screwed his Grace, and so I got your attention. (I no doubt got the Duke of Kent's attention even more.)

Another example:

Booo!!

See? It's an old trick but it works, especially in the world of marketing. Where nobody—*nobody*—has the slightest idea what they're talking about. (Incidentally, they have absolutely no idea that they have no idea what they're talking about. This is what makes them sound so convincing.)

My *arm* just fell off!!!!

Gotcha again!

To sum up, I think I can safely say that in examining the modern-day chronicles of surprise, there is perhaps no surprise greater than the fact that I actually agreed to provide a foreword to this book.

And with it, I have now officially paid off that lingering poker debt, and wish you an enjoyable read. Andy Nulman is not the slightest bit tall, but he makes me laugh. I like him. It will be a surprise to me if you don't. So buy this book. Or you will die.

This Surprisiness of Andy Nulman

Craig Ferguson is an actor, screenwriter, novelist, and comedian, and the host of CBS' Late Late Show.

Andy has a steel-trap commercial mind. He is bright, sharp, and creative. He always has five or six suggestions on any scenario. He has proven to the world, and certainly to me, that he is nothing short of a business genius.

Yet anybody who knows him will tell you that the most surprising thing about Andy is the way he dresses. I have seen him in outfits that range from "transvestite circus performer in a gangster rap video" to what can only be described as "cartoon woodland creature." Why, even though he must be getting close to 50 by now, does he dress so flamboyantly, so unconventionally?

Now you must know I am not a fashion queen; I very rarely notice what other people are wearing. It's just not my thing. I couldn't tell you with any degree of accuracy the color of the underpants I am wearing right now. The point I am trying to make is that I know only one single person in the world open to this kind of scrutiny and it's Andy. He forces you into it. He's just so damned eye-catching. The odd thing is that Andy doesn't see his sartorial eccentricity at all, and I run the risk of hurting his feelings by even mentioning it. But I think it is relevant to the book that you now have in your hands.

Andy is that rare thing in this world—courageous. He is brave to the point of utter foolhardiness as he proves day in and day out, sometimes just with his choice of socks or shirt. He doesn't really entertain the thought of failure, or if he does, he looks on it as a necessary piece of information that he needed to get where he wanted to go.

Of course there may be a darker more Machiavellian reason for Andy's costumes. He might want to trick people into underestimating him.

Trust me, that would be a big mistake.

10 Rather Surprising Things You Should Know About Me Before Reading This Book

- **First of all**, and perhaps most importantly for this book, I walk the talk. Not only have I been Surprise marketing for years, way before the term was even coined, but everything about me screams different and unexpected—the way I dress, the jewelry I wear, the manner in which I talk, the car I drive, and the way I act (even the way I spell Surprise, which is always capitalized out of respect). Some journalist once labeled me "A Somewhat Smarter Smart-Ass," which I didn't mind then, and still don't; another called me "The 3D Kid" (for Does Things Differently). These days, friends and family give me pseudo-serious nicknames like "The Prince of Pow!" and "Mister Surprise." I can think of a lot worse things to be called.

- **On a whim** at the age of 16, I answered an ad to work in the sports section of a newspaper called *The Sunday Express*. A week later, I wrote my first article about the rockstar rage-du-jour at the time, Peter Frampton. A year later, I was named entertainment editor of the paper, and took on the job of promotion manager six months after that. I was well on my way to a life in journalism until I was fired at the age of 23 after throwing a glass of red wine at my white-sweatered boss (I swear it was in self defense! He cut my tie first!). In retrospect, I owe my life to that glass of wine.

- **Laughter is not** just the best medicine, but for 15 years as CEO of the Just For Laughs Comedy Festival, it was my sustenance. It was while building the world's largest humor event that I learned the power of Surprise, and saw it molded like sculptor's clay by the likes of Jerry Seinfeld, Tim Allen, Jim Carrey, Drew Carey, Chris Rock, Ray Romano, John Cleese, William Shatner, Craig Ferguson, and dozens more. Running a comedy event gave me the license to experiment like a mad scientist, and the fallback excuse of "Just kidding!" when I went too far. It was there that I was able to unobtrusively try my hand at producing and writing television shows, directing live shows, and selling everything from multi-million-dollar sponsorships to multi-million-dollar TV series to ten-buck t-shirts.

- **Leaving a posh**, globe-trotting position at Just For Laughs after its best year ever seemed foolish, especially to start up a mobile media/entertainment company called Airborne Entertainment immediately after the dot-com bust. Most people didn't give the company a year to live, but five tough ones later, working with giants like Verizon Wireless, Sprint, AT&T, Disney, HBO, and Fox, my partner and I sold it to a Japanese concern for over $100 million. If I were still a journalist, perhaps I'd be lucky enough to write about this deal. Once again, thank you glass of wine!

- **Outgoing?** Well, somewhat. Somewhat of a paradox, I'd say. I'm okay one-on-one, at my most comfortable onstage in front of crowds as large as 6,000 . . . but suck at parties. Some are party animals; I'm a party vegetable. For some reason, I'd rather go to the dentist than to a party.

- **When I was a kid**, my first career goal was to be a garbage man. Seriously. I was about three-and-a-half years old and looking out from my bedroom window on Westbury Street one night, I saw these guys making a complete racket, throwing large cans around at random, and jumping on-and-off of a moving truck. "What a job!" I remember thinking. "Where do I sign up?"

- **My most beloved** possessions include my ever-expanding wild wardrobe, my music library (including Edison cylinders, 78s, LPs, cassettes, 8-track tapes, CDs, MP3s, and 100 45s locked in a 1959 Wurlitzer jukebox), my pop art collection (with works by Andy Warhol, Roy Lichtenstein, Sol LeWit, Damien Hirst, Ron English, Chuck Close, Salvador Dali, Julien Opie, Patrick Hughes, and Jean-Michel Basquiat), and an assortment of rare, first-edition books.

- **Every now and then**, I let my temper get the best of me. Volcanic in nature, it got the worst of me one summer at Just For Laughs when I trashed my entire office—desk, bookshelves, windows, coffee cups—with a baseball bat. Diane Shatz, my assistant at the time, hid under her desk to escape the flying shrapnel. I'm not necessarily proud of that outburst, but it does make a good story. And that chipped, gnarled bat still sits beside my desk . . . just in case.

- **Though far from** the world's greatest athlete, I work out incessantly, play hockey both weekly and weakly (at the most masochistic of positions, goaltender), and spend my Christmas holidays snowboarding in the west. I have a custom-painted goalie mask (a replica of a famous Stuart Davis mural), a custom-painted snowboard helmet (a laughing, broken skull with gooey brain matter pouring out of the cracks), and select my workout wear to match one of the eight different pairs of training shoes I have. What's a sport without the proper accompanying outfits?

- **One of my few vices** in life is my obsessive love of Cool Whip (particularly Cool Whip Light, which has only 35 calories in three heaping tablespoons!), Kraft's nondairy, neosynthetic, cloud-like whipped topping. I put it on just about everything, even resort to eating it out of the tub, and as an added bonus, let my dogs Shaydee and Rawqui lick the spoon when I'm done. Other than this, I eat pretty healthily. Other vices include coffee, sunglasses, really good red wine, and jewelry.

PROLOGUE
Surprise Drives It Home

"Everybody gets a car!"

In the annals of Surprise marketing (the bulk of which is comprised by the book you are currently holding), those four words rank right up there with Neil Armstrong's symbolic, "That's one small step for a man, one giant leap for mankind" or Ronald Reagan's passionate plea, "Mr. Gorbachev, tear down this wall!"

"Everybody gets a car!"

Shrieked on afternoon TV by Oprah Winfrey on Monday, September 13, 2004, the words served to draw the proverbial "line in the sand," the division of "what came before" and "what came after." To Surprise marketers—the bold, the few—it was the end of BC and the start of AD.

"Everybody gets a car!"

The divine Miss O had done some crazy stuff before (my fave by far saw her symbolize her weight loss by hauling out a Radio Flyer wagon filled with 67 pounds of gooey pink fat), but this one was about to take the cake. There were 276 people in the audience, there to celebrate her wildly successful show's nineteenth anniversary. Some had waited more than five years on a long, long list for their chance to breathe the same air as Oprah, and little did they know when they sat down under the hot Harpo Studio lights that day how well worth it their wait was.

The audience was not there randomly. Each was chosen due to a sob story that they, their friends, or their family had written about their desperate need for a new car. As reported by the Associated Press, one hopeful bemoaned that her car looked "like she got into a gunfight"; another couple talked of driving two vehicles with a combined total of over 400,000 miles. These folks didn't just need a car, they needed a miracle.

And Oprah delivered one . . . at first, for 11 tremulous audience members she called up on stage. Each one was handed the keys to a spanking new Pontiac G6, worth a whopping $28,000. Wild applause was followed by a bit of trepidation as the twelfth and final car's winner was to be decided by lottery. Every one of the remaining 265 anxious fans was given a gift box. One of these boxes contained the keys to the remaining G6.

But upon opening the boxes, the audience got the Surprise of their lives. Every box had a set of keys. And thus. . .

"Everybody gets a car!"

Pandemonium ensued as Oprah repeated the catchphrase over and over again—jumping up and down Tom Cruise-like, for emphasis—to convince her faithful that pinches were not necessary. Yes, this was indeed real. Free cars, donated by the GM brand, a nineteenth anniversary present from Oprah.

The stunned audience didn't just react or overreact, they convulsed. They undulated and writhed. They collapsed. They followed Oprah en masse as if she were Moses as she parted the studio doors and led them to the promised land of the parking lot to claim their Pontiacs, each resplendent with a giant red bow.

Two-hundred and seventy-six ecstatic people and one beaming host. Such is the power of a great Surprise.

But it didn't end there.

The show, appropriately titled "Wildest Dreams," unleashed a maelstrom of attention. According to comScore Networks, a marketing intelligence firm, the Pontiac giveaway drew 600,000 unique American visitors to Oprah.com on Tuesday, September 14, 2004 alone, an increase of more than 800 percent, versus the previous four Tuesdays. Pontiac.com enjoyed a similar jump in visits, up more than 600 percent. More than 48 hours after the show aired, the term "Pontiac G6" was still one of the most popular search items on Google. Within two weeks, the company had achieved an astonishing 87 percent awareness among adults for the G6.

The event's media impact was measured by product placement evaluator iTVX to be equivalent to that of 75 30-second network spots, which the company valued at over $5 million. Even better was that the G6 quickly outsold its nearest competitive vehicle, Ford's 500, by about 20 percent.

Mark-Hans Richer, Pontiac's Marketing Director at the time, shared in the euphoria, and said of the exploit: "It provided a rare chance to fully integrate advertising, product placement, promotion and public relations activities into a single event that created instant, high-impact buzz across America."[1] Surprise conquers a nation.

But wait, there's more.

Nine months later, at the esteemed Cannes Lions d'Or international advertising awards, the Pontiac giveaway went beyond its "Wildest Dreams" and was bestowed with a Golden Media Lion, the event's most prestigious honor. Out of 75 countries participating, this was the only U.S. win. The Pontiac Giveaway was now a global story, a pop-culture phenomenon. "Everybody gets a car!" became part of the common lexicon.

Yeah, yeah, yeah . . . there was also the perfunctory whining and moaning backlash: "Some poor folks were hit with $7,000 tax bills they couldn't pay!" was the gossip that permeated the Internet. (Reports vary; the aforementioned AP story said that "Pontiac will pay for the taxes and the customizing of the cars.") The point is that here we are, five years later, and still talking about it. Say "Pontiac Giveaway" or "Everybody gets a car!" and people know what you mean.

That's the power of a great Surprise.

But there's more still.

As Oprah herself said to describe her bellwether nineteenth "Wildest Dream" season: "This year, no dream is too wild, no Surprise too impossible to pull off."

These days, given her ABC *Big Give* primetime legacy, her "My Favorite Things" product giveaway orgy shows, and her constant dedication to delivering eye-poppers, Oprah reigns as the queen of the Surprise stunt. But with the Pontiac Giveaway, she showed that Surprise can also be a valid marketing tool, crossing over from a world of mere curiosity to one of metered Return on Investment (ROI). Gotta hand it to Oprah; she gave Surprise marketing its first jolt of legitimacy.

This book provides it with its second.

Hang on—and enjoy the ride.

CHAPTER 1
Why Surprise Is Crucial

Three dozen virginal seraphim angels are busy spraying their throats, frantically lining up in choir formation. An army of sweaty Dizzy Gillespies are huffing and puffing their bulbous cheeks, readying for a simultaneous blast of their strangely bent trumpets. The ancient Chinese firework maestro delicately places his bony finger on the ignition switch, itching to flick it forward and light up the skies with explosive rocket color.

Impatiently, they await the triggering event for their synchronized actions—the revelation of this book's "Big Statement." So without any further ado . . .

> *The element of Surprise*
> *is the most important aspect*
> *in contemporary business.*

There—I said it. And now, for the next 200 pages or so, I have to live up to it.

(Uh, angels and company, it's been a pleasure working with you. Your checks are waiting in the dressing rooms. You can all go home now . . . Thank you.)

My quest begins murkily, focusing on the fog that's currently engulfing us. No, it's not the residue of the aforementioned pyrotechnics; it's the thickening cloud of marketing messages we are faced with on a daily basis. Too many messages coming at us in too many places and in too many ways: on TV, radio, in print, and magazines; on billboards, buses, taxis, and racecars. Embedded on web pages, appended to emails and text messages when the emails and text messages themselves aren't ads. Disguised as entertainment and news. Through our front door, over our heads, on sidewalks, and on rooftops. Never mind "ad creep"—this is ad infinitum.

This deluge of messages would be easier to accept if they were clever or inspiring, but sadly, they are not. Most of them are downright boring. The end result is a yawn-inducing, decreasingly effective, peasoup-esque haze.

So, back to the "Big Statement." The marketing message blur, while imposing, is not impenetrable. There indeed exists a beacon powerful enough to slice right through it: the dazzling, halogen-like element of Surprise.

While it recalls the frivolity of birthday parties and the silliness of practical jokes, Surprise is far from superficial. In fact, it is an essential tool that can help you sell anything—your product, your service, even yourself. (Yup, it's as effective in building relationships as it is in building brands, but more on that later.)

Surprise is an ultraimportant form of differentiation. You never really look for it; it finds you. "The moments we enjoy take us by Surprise," said the great anthropologist Ashley Montagu. "It is not that we seize them, but that they seize us."[1] Once it seizes, Surprise helps influence decisions, and is often the deciding factor in someone choosing you over the other guy. But until now, its potential in business has remained relatively untapped.

The perfunctory Google search on Surprise yields an astonishing 159 million hits; page after page of links to something having to do with the good word. While delightful, eye-opening, and uplifting, they seem to be miles away from our corporate cause. For instance:

- Surprise.com brings you "hand-picked gifts from stores across the web."

- There are 32 different international sites for "Kinder-Surprise," the chocolate egg with the toy inside (make sure you chew before you swallow, kids!).

- You can find loads of books on the subject, almost all for children, ranging from *Purim Surprise* by Lesley Simpson to Harriet Ziefert's *Surprise!* (Yeah I know; not much of a range . . .)

- Listen to music by legends like Paul Simon (the album *Surprise*) and Radiohead (the "No Surprises" video), or visit the home pages of unknown bands like To My Surprise, Donner Surprise Party, and My Second Surprise, or indie labels like Surprise Attack Records.

- You can drown in the cesspool of celebrity gossip ("Surprise! Angelina is preggers!").

- Shop at home with Surprise, the French, Avon-like, family fashion company.

- There are countless mentions of Surprise visits, parties, wins, losses, appearances, talks, and comebacks.

- You can discover some very interesting ways to "Surprise" your woman or man (or both).

🍢 Bone up on your history by learning about the American tradition of the October Surprise (a news event, either random or conspiratorially preplanned, with the potential to influence the outcome of an election, particularly one for the presidency), or the 13 ships of the Royal British Navy named the *HMS Surprise*.

🍢 And of course, there's everything you would ever want to know about Surprise, Arizona, a safe little town (only one murder per year on average) with 85,914 residents (including 11 registered sex offenders), where the most common job is construction for males and health care for females, and where the average new single-family home will set you back $159,200. It may not be Manhattan, but Surprise, Arizona is the spiritual homeland of this book (and is a way nicer town than Success, Missouri or Salesville, Ohio).

You'd think that there would be a more reverential treatment of Surprise among the 159 million hits, given the concept's wide-reaching heritage and power. Just look around you. Like Wi-fi, Surprise may be difficult to see, but it is impossible to ignore. In spite of its rather anemic showing on Google, here is where we'll let Surprise really flex its muscles by showing that it is all the following, and more:

The Basis of All Great Entertainment

Think of Surprise endings in classic films like Alfred Hitchcock's *Psycho* (he's his mom!), *Citizen Kane* (it's a sled!), *Planet of the Apes* (it's New York!), *Soylent Green* (it's us!), and *Chinatown* (she's the sister *and* the daughter!). Or more recently, *The Empire Strikes Back* (he's his dad!), *The Crying Game* (she's a he!), *The Sixth Sense* (he's dead!), and *Memento* (it's . . . he's . . . uh, frankly I'm still trying to figure it out). Stop me now, because I could go on and spoil movie endings for pages!

On the smaller screen, there's the TV cliffhangers like *Dallas's* season-ending, "Who Shot J.R.?" episode, its *Simpsons* spoof, "Who Shot Mr. Burns?", or the ever-present twists and turns of shows like *24, Deal Or No Deal*, and *Survivor*.

On the bookshelves, Surprise endings are found in just about anything by Stephen King, Ayn Rand, or my favorite, Joseph Heller's *Catch-22*. (And just wait until you find out how *THIS* book ends . . .)

How about those breakout bands that come from nowhere and capture the nation's attention with an infectious hit song? Or those megastars who generate heaps of publicity by popping up and performing in the strangest places, like the Beatles' rooftop concert in London's Saville Row, the Rolling Stones playing "Brown Sugar" on a flatbed truck through the streets of New York in 1975, or more recently, minishows by Linkin Park and the Jonas Brothers (two separate occasions, trust me!) at the SoHo Apple Store?

Surprise is what separates show business from regular business, a concept explained by actor/director/icon Warren Beatty. Commenting in the *New York Times* he said: "In this Wall Street and corporate world, the discussion has become: 'What is the proven, unique selling property of this product?' The problem is you can't sell entertainment the way you sell cars or air-conditioners. Entertainment is dependent on Surprise."[2]

The Root of All Sports

Where would sports be without Surprise? Extinct, that's where. Imagine if you knew the outcome of the big game in advance; what could possibly inspire you to watch it? (Yeah, the commercials, but the best ones there pop with Surprise as well.)

Ever since David took on Goliath at Judah Field, the inherent unpredictability of sporting battles has given rise to literally thousands of great sports Surprise stories, of unsuspecting heroes, of impossible comebacks, of improbable upsets, of victories snatched from the jaws of defeat (and vice versa). Some of the most memorable include the 1969 "Miracle Mets" World Series win; the Joe Namath Super Bowl boast upset of the Baltimore Colts that same year; or the stunning knockout of previously undefeated heavyweight champ Mike Tyson by journeyman underdog Buster Douglas in 1990. As a die-hard hockey fan, I've got to cite the 1980 U.S. Olympic "Miracle on Ice" hockey team shocking the mighty Russians and then beating Finland for the gold medal (a feat that was not just voted as the biggest sports upset of all time by viewers of ESPN, but cited as the greatest sports moment of the twentieth century by *Sports Illustrated* magazine). These are the stories you tell your kids . . . and sometimes, too often.

Surprise gives sports more than just its dramatic moments—it is its raison d'etre. Sportswriter Bob Duff said it best in an article about the demise of team dynasties, those "sure bets" to win the championship year after year after year: "There are no guarantees, even when games mean the most." I'm sure the almost-perfect 2008 New England Patriots would agree.[3]

Want a guaranteed win? Take in a Harlem Globetrotters game. Or play Solitaire.

The Key to Fashion

Every season, fashionistas line the runways of Milan, Paris, New York, and London in search of answers to momentously important questions like "Long or short?", "Wide or narrow?", "Stripes, solids, or plaids?", "Anorexic or bulimic?", or "What color is the new black?" Mixing up hues, materials, lengths, heights, and widths ensures a continuum of discards and purchases; the lifeblood of the industry.

Like sports, the fashion industry thrives on Surprise. In fact, one of the newest modern-day spectator sports is Celebrity Fashion Scrutiny—who's wearing what, and why. It doesn't just sell clothes, it sells magazines, and draws eyeballs to web sites and TV. Why else do people tune in to the Oscars?

The Difference in Politics

Surprise has reared its head and roared its power in politics ever since the dawn of democracy. Put the outcome of a race in public hands and watch the fun! From the days of "Dewey Beats Truman" (the embarrassing mistake by the *Chicago Daily Tribune*, who printed the expected result of the 1948 presidential election as its front-page headline) to the 2000 Bush-Gore Florida "hanging chad" debacle to 2008's see-saw battle between Democratic candidates Hilary Clinton and Barack Obama (Clinton a sure thing! Obama hot, Clinton toast! Hilary roars back! Obama sweeps! . . . well, you get the picture), followed closely by the Republicans' jaw-dropping decision to plop Alaska Governor Sarah Palin as its VP choice, politics have shocked-and-awed long before George W. Bush decided to visit Iraq.

And it's not just the end results either; the process of getting them also relies heavily on Surprise. To counter a jaded populace who are increasingly nonplussed by tacky attack ads, who don't believe the promises, and who are drop-dead bored by the standard speeches, candidates are creating personal and rather inventive videos to launch their candidacies, to announce their campaign theme songs (Hilary's *Sopranos* closing sequence parody), or to rally the troops (Will.I.Am's "Yes We Can" masterstroke for Obama).

The Underlying Spirit of Web 2.0

I've always said that without the spirit of Surprise, the Internet itself would still be stuck in gear 1.0. Think about this the next time you open an email forwarded to you by a friend: what spreads? The mundane, the usual, the expected? No chance. What "goes viral" are the wild, the unexpected, the unusual and—let's face it—the profane.

Seth Godin, one of the true maestros of the "new marketing," puts it this way: "If you want the word to spread, if you expect me to take action I've never taken before, it seems to me that you need to do something that hasn't been done before. It might not feel safe, but if you do the safe thing, I guarantee you won't Surprise anyone. And if you don't Surprise anyone, the word isn't going to spread."[4]

It used to destroy me when I heard presumably intelligent marketing execs say that their teams are busy cobbling together "a viral video." Get with the program, folks—the public decides what's viral, not the creator. The big-budget corporate endeavors (à la the ill-fated Bud.TV, the $40 million project called "one of the most ambitious-yet-poorly implemented brand forays into online content/video")[5] go embarrassingly ignored while the unheralded, bootstrapped, half-assed, independent eye-poppers like the Diet Coke-Mentos geysers, the supposed cellphone-popped popcorn, or the Blend-Tec scenes of blender destruction rip around the globe like a pandemic.

Surprise is the germ that jumpstarts a Web 2.0 virus; without it, things would spread as rapidly and easily as frozen peanut butter. In a Web 2.0 devoid of Surprise, YouTube would be as interesting as your parents' Super-8 home movies (which are probably also there, but mercifully ignored).

Surprise is also at the foundation of some of Web 2.0's most prolific corporate success stories. Show me the psychic that went out on a limb to predict the meteoric rise of Google or Facebook or MySpace or Ning and I'll show you a liar. (Or a *really lucky* valley venture capitalist.) One of my favorite adages of all time is the skeptical, "He who predicts the future lies . . . even if he tells the truth." You may have high hopes for a new venture, you may show it by placing a big bet on 'em . . . but you never *really* know.

The "Hot" in Hotels

I bring this one up for one main reason: the infamous, sacrilegious Holiday Inn slogan of the 1970s that stated, "The Best Surprise Is No Surprise."

Compare that dreary sentiment to the one espoused by Mari Balestrazzi, Vice President of Design for the Morgan's

Hotel Group, who admits: "One of the company's original ideas was 'hotel as theater' . . . this whole notion of risk-taking and creating environments that are unexpected."[6] Down the street at The Meridien, its Senior Vice President Eva Zeigler has recruited a lineup of artists to come up with everything from limited-edition designer room keys, to hands-on cuisine workshops, to a custom-created cacophonic "soundtrack" to greet customers in the lobby. Why do it? As per Henri Scars Struck, who composed said soundscape: "The goal is to Surprise."[7]

And in an effort to let bygones be bygones, I leave the last word to Peter Gowers, Chief Marketing Officer of the Inter-Continental Hotel Group (IHG), parent company of Holiday Inn: "Our (new) aim is to deliver personalization with personality. You can bring about consistency, but you also get a personal stamp on everything we do."[8] That's one small step for Holiday Inn; one giant leap for Surprise.

❦

Surprise works. It works everywhere. And it works big time. Put simply, Surprise is the difference between a "Holy Jeez!" and a "Who Cares?" And I don't care what you're selling—cool stuff, bold ideas, personal beliefs, political candidates, or just plain you—everything sells better with a "Holy Jeez!"

So back to our murky cloud, or as it shall henceforth be known, "The Murketing Message" (a term I SWEAR I came up with before even hearing about Rob Walker and his book "Buying In"!). I mentioned earlier how people don't believe political promises anymore. Well, in the credibility game, marketing promises don't fare that much better. People distrust marketers (a Yankelovich study in 2007 tore open the wound and said that "76% of consumers don't believe that companies tell the truth in ads").[9] They distrust them so vehemently that if they're not simply ignoring them, they lie to them in surveys, focus groups, and other "intelligence gathering" (2006's Research Industry Summit in Chicago concluded not just that "50% of all survey responses come from less than 5% of the population," but one senior researcher went so far as to say, "We're perpetuating a fraud").[10]

People, however, trust other people. We speak the truth all right, but only behind marketers' backs. And only to others. This is why the power of traditional mass media marketing is rapidly waning, and as a corollary, why the concept of Word Of Mouth Marketing is becoming increasingly vital— and effective. *Really* effective. Forrester Research revealed that "Friends and Family" are more than five times more influential than TV, radio, or newspaper ads.[11] Steve Knox, CEO of Procter and Gamble's Vocalpoint Word of Mouth Marketing division may be less than objective, but he echoes the sentiments of many when he says that "The most powerful form of marketing is an advocacy message from a friend."[12] Despite this, word of mouth (henceforth, WOM) is not a self-starter. It needs a catalyst, a kick-start, something to get it roaring.

Surprise is that something. If WOM is the fuel for today's effective marketing machine, Surprise is the spark that ignites it. And the brighter the spark, the more raging the ensuing inferno.

In the seminal book on the subject, Andy Sernovitz, the former CEO of the Word Of Mouth Marketing Association (every cause has its official governing body), lays down the guiding principle of the genre:

Word of Mouth Marketing isn't about marketers or marketing. It's about real people and why those real people would want to talk about you and your stuff.

Here, here! Or, more appropriately: hear, hear!

In outlining his Four Rules of WOM, Sernovitz validates the need for Surprise. "Rule #1—Be Interesting. Nobody talks about boring companies. Rule #2—Make People Happy. Happy people are your greatest advertisers. Thrill them."[13] No need to even go to numbers three or four: point made.

So Surprise isn't a luxury, but a veritable necessity. And it's more necessary than ever in our brave new world of enlightened, cynical, information-omnivorous consumers. Consumers with more access to more data than any society in history. Consumers who won't accept trade-offs. Consumers who take for granted that everything had better be right, every time . . . and know how to bitch loudly when it ain't.

Author James Surowiecki, best known for his break-through book *The Wisdom of Crowds*, explains how this wisdom translates into some frightening action:

Even as the quality and reliability of products have generally risen, satisfaction ratings have not budged, and in some cases have actually fallen. Businesses are now dealing with buyers who are armed with both information and harsh expectations. In this environment, companies that slip up, even if it's simply failing to match customer tastes, can no longer count on their good names to carry them through. This gives nascent brands an opportunity to succeed, but it also makes staying power a lot harder to come by. Welcome to the 'What Have You Done for Me Lately?' economy.[14]

If that doesn't scare you, listen to this rant from Naomi Wahl, a strategic planner at Ogilvy & Mather, who speaks on behalf of her Gen Y brethren and sistren:

We are in the Age of the Here and the Now. The Age of the Moment to Moment. For you marketers, trying desperately to grab my Gen Y attention as I rush by, here are some tips. Firstly, your brand needs to be the new transformer of our time; capable of renewal and regeneration while demonstrating that essential 'I can't live without you' shiny feature. Next, don't linger. Tell me what you want to tell me, but tell me quickly because I'm already looking in someone else's direction. And finally, be meaningful. Be my hero, and I'll be your rock star.[15]

Yikes! When it comes to price, quality, after-sales service, the shopping experience, guarantees, the whole enchilada, these guys know what they want. They want it all. More than that, they **EXPECT** it all. And there's only one way to please people who expect it all: GIVE THEM WHAT THEY DON'T EXPECT, when they least expect it. Like this:

Welcome back.

By its very definition and nature, Surprise can't be expected, hence its status as a marketer's indispensable secret weapon. The "secret" part is a fundamental distinction, as a regular weapon, no matter how potent, can be defended against if known. It's the sneaky, stealth stuff that ends up kicking your butt when you're not looking. Or, in the words of feared Prussian military strategist Karl Von Clausewitz, who knew a thing or two about weapons, "The backbone of Surprise is fusing speed with secrecy."[16]

And let me tell you, these days, marketers need all the weapons they can get their hands on. The game of persuasion has never been an easy one, but Life 2.0 has made things particularly tricky for professional persuaders, especially when you consider the current status of the media, which has seen its primary function converted from reflective to predictive. In their book *The Deviant's Advantage: How Fringe Ideas Create Mass Markets*, futurists Watts Wacker and Ryan Mathews describe the 180-degree shift in the dissemination of information:

> *When most of us were young, news organizations prided themselves on their ability to accurately report on what had happened. Today, more and more space is being devoted to what they believe* **will** *happen. That's why most of us walk around with a vague feeling of déjà vu. By the time something actually happens, we've read, heard or seen it, generally several times. Ever since Watergate, significant news stories have been "broken" by news leakers rather than news makers.*[17]

With broadcast tools like video cameras, voice recorders, and publishing platforms democratized, omni-accessible, and ultracheap; with citizen journalists running rampant everywhere, blogging, vlogging, and podcasting, these days everybody knows everything—or seems to. Appropriately named "Spoiler Sites" (these web sites divulge inside info on films and TV shows long before they're meant to be known by the general public) are sprouting up on the Net like genetically modified weeds. "Spoiler sites are for people who can't read a book without skipping ahead to the final page," SpoilerFix.com's Isabelle Roy told *Entertainment Weekly*. "We live in a world where everything is instantaneous. We want answers now."

The result, as per film director J.J. Abrams, is that "People think they've experienced things before they really have."[18] What's worse, armed with this information, they often use it as a preemptive aggressive strike. An article in the *Globe and Mail* newspaper about how early Internet buzz tainted and basically sunk the premiere of "Gone With The Wind," a highly touted British stage musical, pondered: "In the blogging age, is it possible to launch a spectacle that will surprise?"[19]

Well, the answer is yes, it is. Great Surprise isn't easy to generate, but it's worth the payoff. It's not brain surgery, but it sure 'nuff is a brain workout. Done right, Surprise delivers that special reaction, one I have coined "***The Pow! Moment***." It's when your heart skips a beat, you're overcome with that special little tingle . . . and you can't wait to see what happens next.

Pow! Moments don't merely generate delightful astonishment from your customers, they solidify the bond between you and them. And I don't care **WHAT** business you are in, from a mom-and-pop corner store to a multinational, there is **NOTHING** more important than the bond between you and your customer. Find a way to eternally concretize this bond and you'll never have another business worry. Ever.

But "eternal customer concretization" is easier said (even five times fast) than done. Like Crazy Glue, the Pow! Moment solidifies these bonds faster. It activates the intersect set, when Surprisor and Surprisee become one. If that sounds a little mutant, don't fret. In Surprise marketing, everything is somewhat askew. We live to defy conventional wisdom; to Surprise marketers, two in the bush is worth more than a bird in the hand—way more. We don't fear the unknown, we embrace it, and exploit it unabashedly.

I saw this in action a couple of years ago at a fundraising event at the Hyatt Regency Hotel in Dallas, Texas. It was at the annual NHL All-Star Game, more specifically the Garth Brooks Teammates for Kids Foundation Gala. After a concert by Trisha Yearwood, a fast-talking Chicago-based auctioneer took to the stage, surrounded by some gleaming, high-profile, big-ticket items up for bid. There were two new Dodge Nitro SUVs, a custom NHL-painted motorcycle made by the Teutul boys of *Orange County Choppers*, an all-expenses paid trip to see Garth perform in a Las Vegas show and have a private dinner with him afterwards, as well as the perfunctory signed original art and hockey memorabilia.

So guess which prize attracted the most feverish bidding? Would you believe ... *an empty envelope*? It was a great lesson in Surprise 101. The auctioneer held up an envelope, showed there was nothing in it, and started bidding at a couple hundred bucks. For about five seconds, nothing happened. The room was silent and perplexed.

Then the crowd, figuring there had to be some sort of golden catch, started a bidding frenzy. All over the vast Landmark Ballroom, hands popped up and waved fervently, looking like some sort of fantasy-land, appendage forest. The silver-haired auctioneer, a seasoned pro, could hardly catch his breath keeping up with the rising total. When it all died down, he had raised close to $5,000. For nothing.

Well, actually, not for nothing. The winner took home a bunch of signed memorabilia; essentially leftovers from the silent auction that took place earlier in the evening in the hotel's hallway.

The winner loved it. The crowd loved it. And I suspect Garth's Foundation didn't mind it either.

It may be scary, but exploring and exploiting the unknown provides disproportionate returns. The reward is worth the risk. If you're willing to take the risk.

Putting faith in Surprise can turn yesterday's fish-wrapped news into today's neon headlines. Just ask the people over at Nintendo. A pioneer in the videogame industry, Nintendo became a tired afterthought at the turn of the twenty-first century, playing a distant third fiddle to the whiz-bang wonders of Sony's Playstation and Microsoft's Xbox. Going head-to-head against them was suicide, so Satoru Iwata, Nintendo's president and CEO, took a different route. He introduced the radical Wii entertainment system, with a simple, human-motion-capturing control, which eschewed the industry's traditional hard-core gamer audience and went after regular folk, like yours truly.

When I first had the chance to try the game in the summer of 2005, in a preview setting at the annual Licensing Show in New York, I was astounded. As a guy who hadn't played videogames in over a decade due to the complexity of button-pushing and sequence-remembering, I was blown away at how easy and intuitive it was. In ten seconds, I was playing video tennis, and playing it well. In essence, Nintendo reinvented the videogame experience from scratch.

"We are not competing against Sony or Microsoft," said Iwata of the gaming market at the time. "We are battling the indifference of people who have no interest in videogames."[20] "Wii was unimaginable for them. And because it was unimaginable, they could not say they wanted it. If you are simply listening to requests from the customer, you can satisfy their needs, but you can never Surprise them."[21]

But Surprise them Iwata did. In a major way. He gave people what they didn't expect. Certainly when they least expected it. And the people responded in kind; in the first six months of direct competition with Microsoft and Sony, Wii outsold Xbox 360 on a two-to-one basis, and crushed Playstation 3 by a four-to-one margin.

The media, unanimously dubious prior to Wii's coming-out party (sticking its tongue out at its old-school graphics and mocking the system's seemingly unpronounceable name), soon swooned all over Nintendo. In a *Fortune* magazine piece from June 2007, writer Jeffrey M. O'Brien gushed:

Nintendo has shown a knack for leapfrogging its industry. Sure, some initiatives failed but the company rarely fails to Surprise. This time, in changing perceptions of gaming, Nintendo has surprised even itself.[22]

O'Brien also spoke to Nintendo's legendary videogame designer Shigeru Miyamoto, the soul of the company for decades (he gave the world superstars like the Super Mario Brothers, Donkey Kong, and the characters from *Legend of Zelda*), and the intellectual driving force behind Wii: "What I want to do," envisioned Miyamoto, "is to make it so people can actually feel something unprecedented." Feel something unprecedented. A somewhat more poetic way to say Pow! Moment, don't you think?

It's not just Nintendo and the wacky world of games. Pow! Moments are being popped by some of America's more traditional, mall-based businesses. OfficeMax's SVP Marketing and Advertising Bob Thacker (responsible for creating the world's largest rubber band ball and the mega-hit "Elf Yourself" viral Christmas Internet campaign) cites "Unexpected events" as his company's two-word marketing strategy.

Then there's the ubiquitous Apple. Even those critical of the company's heavy-handed, secretive, closed-source ways are still impressed with its Pow! Moments. "Part of the joy of being an Apple customer is anticipating the surprises that Santa Steve brings at Macworld Expo every January," wrote journalist Leander Kahney in a tough look at Steve Jobs in *Wired* magazine.[23]

Meanwhile, stalwarts like ol' faithful Procter and Gamble are also jumping aboard the Surprise Express. The company's CEO, A.G. Lafley, who took the moribund old-school behemoth and turned it into a cutting-edge innovation breeding ground, boasts: "Three billion times a day, P&G brands touch the lives of people around the world. Our goal is to delight consumers at two 'moments of truth': First, when they buy a product and second, when they use it."[24]

Three billion Pow! Moments a day? Be still my beating heart! Okay, that may be a little excessive, but the dream of Surprise becoming part of business's standard operating procedure is not unrealistic. And here's why. By now, we all know that the Internet has rewritten all the rules about commerce. As British computer scientist Gavin Potter notes: "The twentieth century was about sorting out supply; the twenty-first is going to be about sorting out demand."[25] *Wired* magazine is even blunter in making the point: "The Internet makes everything available, but mere availability is meaningless if the products remain unknown to potential buyers."[26]

Surprise gets things known. It gets things talked about. And it gets things sold. So look around us again. That fog seems to be lifting a bit. The Murketing Message focus is improving. I'm no Johnny Nash, but I can see clearly now. The rain is gone.

The beam of Surprise is cutting through, and it beckons. Let's see where it takes us.

Summary

THE CRUCIAL STUFF CHAPTER 1 WANTS YOU TO REMEMBER

- Main point: Surprise is the most important aspect in contemporary marketing.

- It's also the reason we watch TV shows, movies, and sports; buy clothes; vote; pass along racy emails; and stay in cool hotels.

- Slash! It slices through the dreariness of the dreaded Murketing Message.

- Talk-generator. It is the spark to the flame that is Word Of Mouth marketing.

- Equation to remember: Two in the bush is worth more than the bird in the hand.

CHAPTER 2
What Is This Thing Called Surprise?

Okay, so we've established that Surprise is crucial. Now we have to work on establishing Surprise itself. What is Surprise? In seeking out a scholarly answer to this "meaning of life"-ish question, I've done my homework, and have scaled the equivalent of Himalayan peaks in books, magazines, library shelves, and web-based research documents in the quest for sage-like clarification. While I have enjoyed the learning process, the overall effect of the journey has made me feel much like legendary ad man David Ogilvy.

You see, David was a pioneer in this industry, way back when marketing guys smoked pipes and wore ascots (think of TV's *Mad Men* with a touch more class). As the founder of the heralded Ogilvy & Mather Agency, he set new standards, took ads in adventurous new directions, and was thus fawned upon as "the pope of modern advertising" by his peers. Yet when winning the American Marketing Association's illustrious Parlin Award, he acknowledged sheepishly:

> *I thought they were kidding. I cannot even understand what the experts write on the subject (of*

marketing). Stuff like this from Professor Paul Warshaw of McGill—"Though use of sample cross-validated correlations is acceptable, the infrequently-used squared cross-validated correlation coefficient is a more precise (although slightly biased) measure. It uses all available data simultaneously rather than bisecting the sample into arbitrary estimation and holdout components . . ."[1]

If a world-renowned thinker like David Ogilvy can admit to being utterly bamboozled by those words about his field of passion (ironically, written by one of my favorite professors during my student tenure at McGill University), I guess I shouldn't feel shame in having my brain explode after reading the following from this groundbreaking 2005 University of Southern California (USC) study about Surprise, sponsored to the tune of $600,000 by the National Science Foundation:

The concept of Surprise is central to sensory processing, adaptation and learning, attention, and decision making. Yet, until now, no widely-accepted mathematical theory existed to quantify Surprise elicited by stimuli or events, for observers ranging from single neurons to complex natural or engineered systems. We have developed a formal Bayesian definition of Surprise that is the only consistent formulation under minimal axiomatic assumptions. We propose that Surprise is a general, information-theoretic concept, which can be derived from first principles and formalized analytically across spatio-temporal scales, sensory modalities, and, more generally, data types and data sources . . .[2]

Yowzah! Help! Massive mind-matter spillage! Mop on aisle four! Mop on aisle four!

Professors Pierre Baldi, Laurent Itti, and Douglas Muñoz, the authors of the USC study, define Surprise as "the distance between the posterior and prior distributions of beliefs over models."[3] Uh, okay. For a whole lot less than six hundred grand, as I wipe the excesses of academia from my hands, allow me to offer a more accessible definition, one that we will use from here on in.

Surprise: The Constant Expansion of the Boundaries of Delightful Extremes.

In a world of standards, sameness, cookie-cutters, and monotony, it's the extreme that stops people in their tracks. It's what people remember. And, more importantly for our businesses, it's what people talk about. In *The Black Swan*, Nassim Nicholas Taleb's study of unpredictable events, the scholar and essayist endorses the extreme as an essential social launch pad:

> *Living on our planet today requires a lot more imagination than we are made to have. Our world is dominated by the extreme, the unknown, and the very improbable, and all the while we spend our time engaged in small talk, focusing on the known, and the repeated. This implies the need to use the extreme event as a starting point.*[4]

The starting point for Surprise is right between your eyes—literally. At its core, Surprise is one of the seven basic human facial expressions. Go ahead, grab a mirror, and act it out. (While you're at it, stretch out your features and try the other six of the family as well: contempt, anger, disgust, fear, sadness, and happiness.)

But more than just another complicated combination of muscle movements, there's a biological purpose to the expression of Surprise. In their book *Unmasking the Face*, Dr. Paul Ekman and Wallace Friesen describe what they call "The Surprise Brow." This, they explain, "is our body's way of forcing us to see more. When our brows go up, it widens our eyes and gives us a broader field of vision."[5]

It doesn't stop at the eyes, though. "Surprise causes our jaws to drop and our mouths to go gape," Ekman and Friesen continue. "We're struck momentarily speechless." Something like Figure 2.1 shows here.

Figure 2.1 Just waiting to be sold something.

Brows up, eyes popped, mouth open, but no sound coming out—not exactly the prettiest of pictures, to say the least. Certainly not the look you want for your graduation photo. Or for your wedding album. But it's still way better than the No-Surprise face, epitomized so perfectly in the US Postal Service ad pictured in Figure 2.2.

Figure 2.2   Go ahead. Make his day. Good luck . . .

To a marketer though, when you rearrange your facial features into the contortion of the Surprise Brow, you have never looked better. This visage makes marketers rearrange their facial features into one of a beaming smile, and gives them the opening they've been waiting to pounce upon.

The Surprise face is bold and attractive on the surface, but it's what's inside that really counts. Dive through the open mouth, reach deep and go for the gut, then take advantage of that special feeling that only Surprise can spawn, one that I call "Euphoric Shock." To best understand the sensation of Euphoric Shock, let's mentally visit a casino. Think of how your body reacts when the roulette ball comes to a full stop in the hole of the number you just played, or when three red cherries line up in a jackpot row on your slot machine. Now imagine that feeling without the precursor of putting down a bet or pulling a lever. Euphoric Shock is a cause-and-effect relationship where the cause is hidden, and controlled by someone else. This hidden cause jumpstarts a modern marketing relationship by "upsetting" one's system, putting it into a state of flux. This mildly alarming internal stirring and accompanying euphoria reduces resistances and thus makes one more susceptible to an impending sales message.

Chip and Dan Heath describe this in greater detail in their best-selling book, *Made to Stick*. They say that "our schemas are like guessing machines. Schemas help us predict what will happen, and consequently, how we should make decisions. Surprise jolts us to attention. (It) is triggered when our schemas fail, and it prepares us to understand why the failure occurred.

"When our 'guessing machines' fail," they continue, "Surprise grabs our attention so that we can prepare them for the future. That extra attention and thinking sears unexpected events into our memories. [And] unexpected ideas are more likely to stick."[6]

Attention is Surprise's legal tender. And its ascent in international currency markets comes at an opportune time, as much of marketing's ol' reliable means of measurement are losing value faster than that retirement property you bought in Florida for $5,000 down. *Advertising Age*'s Teressa Iezzi even suggests a new unit of measurement for attention, the CPU—Cultural-Penetration Units—which she explains are "an amalgam of a range of brand-creativity feedback mechanisms: Internet views and parodies, talk-show/national-news/entertainment-show mentions, likelihood of awareness from siblings/aunts/parents, and other indicators."[7]

Max Levchin, a cofounder of PayPal who started the meteoric-rising web widget company Slide, predicts that in the very near future, "The metrics for success are going to shift away from 'who can provide the most reach' to 'who is paid the most attention.'"[8]

Max makes a key distinction—attention isn't given, it's *paid*. And paid attention is even more important since it's being paid in a world where price points are plunging dangerously and rapidly. In his most recent book, entitled *Free*, Chris Anderson (of *The Long Tail* fame) proposes that the most prevalent price point for business in the future is that most round of numbers, zero. "*Free*'s argument," summarized a piece on Anderson in the marketing magazine *Brandweek*, "is that in the digital age, it is more important to get attention than immediate payoff."[9]

Good point, but eventually, to stay alive and benefit from all this wondrous attention, there has to be some sort of payoff. And that's where Surprise delivers the goods. Yes, it draws attention. It raises brows, pops eyes, and opens mouths. It slices through schemas and shocks euphorically. But most importantly, Surprise makes it easier for people to buy into what you're trying to sell. A happy, excited customer makes less demands, asks less questions, and is almost completed by consummating a transaction with you. This is why I have nicknamed it "The Lubricant to Yes."

"Yes"—there's nothing more that marketers want to hear than that word. It's the sweetest sound of 'em all, a three-letter symphony, the universal key that opens all locks and removes all shackles. You can yammer on all day long, spout the traditional marketing idiom of customer retention, building community, unaided recall, blah, blah, blah all you want, but in the end, no other term matters more than "Yes." But with apologies to Harvard Negotiation Project's Roger Fisher, when it comes to getting to yes, too many marketers choose the wrong roads. They get in your face too quickly and spew spittle as they talk too fast. They pounce on you like starving vultures when you enter their place of business, and spam you for eternity once you leave. In an article in *The Economist* last year, Joe Staton, the head of JWT's Knowledge Center, grumbled about the state of the economy and blurted out the obvious: "Selling people things has become more difficult than it has ever been."[10] And for good reason. People don't want to be sold.

When I was running the Just For Laughs Comedy Festival, I was deluged with hundreds of phone calls, emails, letters, and packages every week by well-meaning but insanely overbearing agents and managers, all trying to push their clients with bribes, threats, promises, and oodles of dubious achievements like, "Everyone knows him! He's the second hamburger in that hot new Wendy's TV spot!"

And I told them all the same thing. Over and over again: "Don't try to sell me; just make it easy for me to buy. Let me discover your product, service, or offer. Don't make me feel that somehow, it was forced on me. Don't, not even for a millisecond, make me feel that the decision was yours, and not mine."

I encouraged a somewhat "antimarketing" approach, one that sells by not selling. Give me just enough eye-popping, eyebrow-raising info to make me want to come to you to buy. This approach has indeed gained credence since I sat in the Festival high chair. Sales guru Jeffrey Gitomer has built a career—an industry, some may say—by promoting the credo, "People don't like to be sold, but they love to buy." (Yikes! He's even trademarked it. Send lawyers, guns, and money!) And buy they will. If you're gentle—and crafty.

So back to our squeeze tube of Surprise lube. "Yes" is where we want to, **NEED** to, get to. So stop pushing people. Instead, make it easy for them to pull. Delight 'em first . . . they'll buy later. Simple, right? So why then do so many people screw it up?

Sorry to say that the concept of Surprise is taken in vain way more often than the Lord's name. It is misused more often than prescription drugs by teens at a weekend-long rave, and is more misunderstood than the lyrics to "Louie Louie." For example, take the city of St. Louis (no relation to the song). In early 2008, the city—one I travel to and love, by the way—embarked on an expensive marketing campaign, buying full-page ads in business magazines, touting itself to meeting planners. In said ads, the Midwestern metropolis labels itself as "Surprising." Fair enough, until . . .

Snap quiz: When you think of St. Louis, what pops into your mind?

- Budweiser beer

- The Blues (the musical style and perhaps even the hockey team)

☛ Baseball's Cardinals and football's Rams

☛ The great Arch

So guess what appears in the "Surprising" ad? A bar scene featuring two-piano blues on stage, Busch Stadium (killing the beer and sports reference with one picture), and the Arch, which is craftily woven into the "St. Lou is Surprising" headline. And the pièce de résistance—a generic picture of the Convention Center/Casino that looks like a candidate for Best in Show at StockPhoto.com. What were they thinking? The imagery is about as Surprising as Florida sunshine or Denver snow. Take away the words "St. Louis" and the Bud logo, and this could be an ad for any major city on the continent.

Here's another misappropriation. About a year ago, I heard a radio ad for Kia Motors, the South Korean car manufacturer, which used the words, "The Power to Surprise" as its tagline. I immediately rushed over to the company's web site, ready to have my system shocked and my "Yes-es" lubricated. So I clicked and I flicked 'til my wrist got numb, but I still didn't hear no cylinders hum. Here's what I found, and I quote:

> The "Power to Surprise" represents Kia's global commitment to surpassing customer expectations through continuous automotive innovation while epitomizing the exciting and enabling values of the Kia brand. Everything we do at Kia, from providing one of the best warranties in the business, having more standard features, or enabling someone to have a car in the first place, is done with this

in mind. Throughout a full line of cars, from the all-new Rio—the most affordable four door sedan in America, to the reintroduced Sportage sport utility vehicle, and now the totally redesigned Sedona minivan, Kia demonstrates its ability to achieve The Power to Surprise ...[11]

You still awake?

And if so, are you thinking what I'm thinking? Sure does sound like the proverbial "same ol' same old," doesn't it? Over-stuffed with graying buzzwords that have stopped buzzing a long time ago. (Hey Kiafolk, there's a sale on adjectives over at Thesaurus.com. Go crazy.) What's worse, the words are imprisoned in a site that's generic and standard; completely colorless and void of personality. The whole experience does to Surprise what Paris Hilton does to fame—devalues the concept.

Now if Kia—which actually makes impressive, well-priced cars—truly embraced the element of Surprise, its radio ads would wobble our earlobes. Its site would be popping with trapdoors, Easter eggs, and a vibrant design that will make us feel, "I gotta check these guys out!" Instead, you'd think this stuff was being produced in North Korea, with Kim Jung Il as Chief Marketing Officer. The Power to Surprise? Not yet. To convince the American consumer, Kia has a long way to go. Better fill up that gas tank, folks.

The Boundaries of Delightful Extremes are like a giant door frame, with you in the middle pushing outward on each side. They can be imposing and confining, but to generate Surprise, you've got to keep pressing on. Go to the gym. Better still, channel the rage of Samson bookended by those giant marble columns. The push isn't easy, but it's imperative if you ever want to break through and send your constraints crashing to the ground.

Unlike the city of St. Louis and Kia Motors, some companies have the guts to embrace the push so profoundly that Surprise becomes ingrained into their genetic makeup. They don't just walk the talk, they run it—in both marathon and sprint style.

One of my favorite examples comes from a Singapore beverage company, quite fittingly named Out Of The Box. Forward-thinking and shrewd, they released two soft drink brands called "Anything" and "Whatever," ostensibly as non-committal responses to the question "What do you wanna drink?" "Anything" is carbonated and comes in a half-dozen flavors (Cola with Lemon, Apple, Fizz Up, Cloudy Lemon, and Root Beer), as does the noncarbonated, tea-based "Whatever" (Ice Lemon, Peach, Jasmine, White Grape, Apple, and Chrysanthemum).

The drinks live up to their names, and literally so—the cans are simply labeled Anything or Whatever, resplendent with a generic list of ingredients that gives nothing away to the thirsty. But this tactic is more than a clever naming convention. The Surprise comes when potential drinkers pop open the can, as they have no idea what they're about to guzzle. Anything and Whatever are like blind dates for your mouth; your taste buds find out the flavor firsthand (or first tongue, perhaps). Talk about Pow! Moments; the Out Of The Box company has converted the common soft drink experience into both a game and an adventure in Surprise.

So has Liquidation World, an off-price retailer found throughout Canada and in Washington state. Despite its status as a deep discounter, Liquidation World is making its mark by underplaying price and overemphasizing Surprise. The company's internal market research revealed that what truly lured customers to their stores was not the potential savings but the opportunity to browse and explore, desperately seeking something they're not really looking for. Taking this to heart, Liquidation World focused its marketing on promoting the experience of finding an unexpected deal, rather than on diminished price points. Today, the company's TV commercials end with the tag line, "Come Find Something Unexpected," while its in-store posters shout out, "Even *We're* Surprised by What People Find in Our Store," and "Find Exactly What You're *Not* Looking For." It ain't about the search, it's about the find.

Surprise isn't only for gutsy little mavericks. It's equally as effective a tool for corporate giants as well. Well, for those risky corporate giants with playful vision and the gumption to act on it rather than just look. Take Target, for example. These guys have become the golden child of both Wall Street and Main Street by mixing the spirit of Wal-Mart with the showiness of the Museum of Modern Art and the madness of Cirque du Soleil. From its eclectic product selection to a barrage of attention-grabbing feats, Target keeps pushing the boundaries (even going as far as stealthily suggesting its name be pronounced the somewhat pretentiously French way: "*Tar-jhay*"). The ensuing results don't merely make noise; events like a floating temporary store in the Hudson River in 2002 or a "vertical fashion show" in 2005, where acrobat models actually walked down the side of New York's iconic Rockefeller Center, earn the company upwards of $7 billion a year in free publicity. Talk about attention being paid. Worth a few brainstorming sessions, don't you think?

A 2008 article in *Fortune* about Target outlined its deep commitment to the flow of Surprise:

> *To encourage, or rather ensure, a steady stream of bold new ideas, managers with a proven record of hits must duke it out for portions of their budgets every year. So although the events team won a big chunk of the 2007 pie with its idea for a holographic fashion show, it had to come up with something equally compelling if it wanted funding this year. That element of Surprise, it turns out, has been part of Target's DNA for some time.*[12]

Any company can pull off some sort of one-off "stunt," but real corporate longevity, customer loyalty, and buzz with a long, serpent-like tail of zzz's come when a company maintains the consistency of delight. Is it any wonder that Target's been around for close to a half-century?

Intimidated yet? Don't be. The beauty of great Surprise is that there is no direct correlation between size of the event and the amount of Pow! it can generate. Little things indeed mean a lot, and can spawn a disproportionate amount of shock and ahh! (You'll learn just how important little things are when we look at them in detail in Chapter 6.) The Return on Investment (ROI) measure here is "Return on Interest" generated; the actual ROI takes a backseat for a spell. Three years ago at Christmastime, while waiting in a rather long line to pay for books at the Chapters Bookstore in Toronto, I was tapped on the shoulder by one of its employees, decked out in a Santa hat and a wide smile. Her mission? Not to sell me a "frequent buyer" card or to solicit charitable funds, but to offer me a chocolate from an overflowing basket of edible holiday goodies.

"We've had long lines all day," she said. "And this will help take your mind off waiting."

No thanks, I said, pointing to the jeans I was trying to keep at size 30. Bad for the waistline. But great for this book.

See what I mean? Something as simple as offering waiting customers a tiny treat they weren't expecting can lead to a story that's published in a best-selling business book years later. And when I give my frequent speeches on the subject of Surprise, this story is recounted once again. Go figure how many thousands of people have heard about Chapters Books because someone decided to spend 10 bucks one night and do something for the poor souls waiting in line.

When I ran Just For Laughs, I made sure that we did something like this for the insanely long lines outside the box-office the first day we put our shows on sale. We had roving performers telling jokes, we held dopey contests, gave away t-shirts and other swag. The "line-tertainers" had as much fun as those whose wait was lessened by this attention-attracting, delay deflector. Come to think of it, I don't know why more companies don't do this at other places where they find their customers delayed and standing in line formation, like airports, border crossings, or movie theaters.

Another example of small act/big effect is the card I found in a laundry bag on my bed at the London NYC Hotel during a recent stay. Instead of the standard, "Put Your Shoes in the Bag for a Complimentary Shoeshine" notice, the hotel offers what they call a "Workout Wear Refresher." To wit:

*For complimentary cleaning of your workout wear,
place your clothing in the laundry bag with this card
and touch 62 for pickup before 10 am. Clothing will
be returned by 5 pm.*

This may not be for everyone, but for those of us who choose their hotels by their gym and spa facilities, this helps facilitate the choice. And for a guy who obsessively trains, this is a godsend. Instead of packing multiples of shorts, socks, t-shirts, and bandannas, one set is enough for my morning shvitz every day (well, when I stay at this hotel, at least). Speaks volumes about the hotel's hip target market too, who are apt to be wearing more sneakers than wingtips, and about the cost of running a shoeshine operation . . . or the declining demand for it. I guess workouts are the new shoe polish. (And I'm sure if I *really* needed a shoeshine, the London NYC would get me one.)

It's not that a hotel's standard shoeshine offer (or the chocolate on the bed, or the next day's weather prediction) is bad, it's just that it's been done—and so often that it's now expected and predictable. Nobody's going to use a hotel shoeshine as a catalyst to Word Of Mouth marketing. But I know of a half-dozen people I have personally influenced to stay at the London NYC (mad chef Gordon Ramsey's inaugural American restaurant in the lobby doesn't hurt either; frankly, its mouthwatering tasting menu was one of the reasons I HAD to work out while there). As music theorist Brian Eno once said, "It's almost impossible to know which grain of sand is going to start an avalanche."[13]

Obviously, anything Surprising can't be predictable. Predictability is the antithesis of Surprise. But to really hit home, a Surprise has to be, to borrow a fresh buzzword from the

Heath Brothers, "*Post*-dictable." As they explain: "To be satisfying, a Surprise must be post-dictable. Great Surprise endings unite clues that you've been exposed to all along. The twist makes sense after you think about it, but it's not something you would've seen coming."[14]

Ahh, the twist. Not à la Chubby Checker, but the one at the root of all things funny. No wonder I've become so obsessed with the element of Surprise—it shares the same foundation as the element of humor, which has long been part of my heritage. During the 1990s, given my credentials as the Comedy Festival CEO, I was asked to bring some of it to the classroom and teach a university-level course in humor writing. Over the semester, the course became extremely detailed and granular, but I used the entire two hours of the first class to explain just one thing—the most basic building block of all comedy, the basic blueprint for every joke: the "fork in the Road" theory.

In essence, it works like this. Every joke begins as a journey. The teller takes his or her audience by the hand and leads them down a playful path. They walk for a bit (the set-up) until they reach a juncture, the proverbial "fork in the road." At that point, the teller subtly offers the audience a sneak peek at their ultimate destination; that place in the distance at the end of the right-hand turn. But the humor comes when the teller suddenly and abruptly hauls the audience the other way, taking the left-hand turn down the unexpected route (also known as the punch line).

The joke I always used as a practical example to accompany this theory was the classic, "What's black and white and red (read) all over?" Given the set-up hues of black and white, the audience hears "read" as the color red, thinks kaleidoscopically, and conjures up right-hand turns of Santa Claus in a tar pit, chocolate sundaes with cherry sauce, and bleeding zebras. The left-hand turn twist, the punch line, comes upon hearing the answer: "A newspaper," where the "read" is now understood to be the verb used to connote reading. Please, hold onto your sides!

Still with me? Yeah, sometimes the students kinda dozed off as well (one of the great adages about humor is that learning how to put together a joke is like learning how to put together sausage—you love the end result, but knowing what goes into it is best left a mystery). However, the students' understanding of this simple theory helped them create literary magic, and breathe new lives of laughter into the most stillborn of noncomedic premises.

Humor and Surprise—brothers in arms, or cousins, at least. Their respective facial expressions of delight are also from the same family (Happiness is also one of the Seven Basics), except that laughing narrows out Surprise's popped eyes, and elongates its O-shaped mouth. Given the worldwide love of humor, and its oft-cited healing power, you'd figure that this relationship would be a good one for Surprise.

Unfortunately, it's not. You can choose your friends, but not your family. And being kinfolk with humor has somewhat diminished Surprise's reputation. The next chapter will help restore it, and be explained in a way that even David Ogilvy could understand.

Summary

THE STUFF CHAPTER 2 WANTS TO ESTABLISH

- Remember the definition: Surprise is the constant expansion of the boundaries of delightful extremes.

- Surprise is also one of the Seven Basic Facial Expressions (along with Contempt, Anger, Disgust, Fear, Sadness, and Happiness). Pop those eyes and raise those brows!

- Understand the Surprise economy's financial model—attention is paid, and invaluable.

- Revitalize your vocabulary with these snappy Surprise terms: "Euphoric Shock" and "The Lubricant to Yes."

- Post-dictability is a key to satisfaction; you may not see Surprise coming, but it has to make perfect sense once it does.

CHAPTER 3
What Surprise *Ain't*

When I was a little boy, no more than four years old, my mom gave me some great life advice: Don't talk to strangers. Last year, while taking a train instead of the usual plane to a speaking engagement, I finally understood why.

The reason I had chosen the train in the first place was to get in an uninterrupted five-hour writing block, during which I would cocoon myself and compose a few posts for the "Pow! Right Between the Eyes" blog that paved the way for this book. Sadly, my naive utopian fantasy was shattered less than an hour after leaving the station.

"Whatcha writing about?" said the woman next to me as she peered over my shoulder and onto my laptop.

Normally, I would try to deflect such unsolicited queries into the outskirts of oblivion—at very least, into the next car—but I felt bad for my nosy seatmate, as 20 minutes prior to this intrusion, the train's Steward spilled a full cup of hot coffee onto her lap (an episode I later cynically labeled, "Pow! Right Between the Crotch"). Feeling for her misfortune, I acquiesced, and told her I was writing some posts for my blog on the power of Surprise.

Incredulous, Ms. Sitting-Next-To-Me blurted out: "You write a blog based on that? You mean, 'Surprise Parties' and 'Gotcha!' and jumping out of a cake and all that stuff?"

"Uh, yeah," I replied somewhat defensively. What I **should have** said . . . is this chapter. Despite its innocent-enough moniker and joyous Technicolor image, Surprise is far from frivolous. In fact, to work—particularly in the business and personal relationship framework I have set it within—it has to be rather profound. The Surprise that truly connects, that unites its sender and recipient, is rife with meaning.

And not just "meaning" in a pedantic, academic sense. "Meaning" as in something that permeates the spirit and lives in the soul. Meaning, which was deftly defined by the *Atlantic Monthly* as "the catalyst that turns action into drama . . . a sense that action is leading to some transformation or resolution."[1]

Now *that's* what Surprise is all about. So throw those kiddie-colored glasses into the toy box, and let's start looking at this like adults. And perhaps the best way to do that is to focus not on what Surprise is, but what it ain't.

In discussing the nature of this book with colleagues and marketing peers, what seemed to come up most often is the notion of "Surprise as Service." "Treat people better than they expect," said a retailer at the Shop.org conference in Orlando last year during a chin-wag about Surprise, "then they'll never forget you, and keep coming back."

Maybe they will. While it works as part of a greater package, on its own the concept of service is rather overrated. Given enough time and patience, slaves and robots can be taught to serve well, as could some clever dogs who can even-tually fetch your slippers, newspapers, and/or cans of beer.

While Surprise is indeed a catalyst that can form a permanent bond between you and your customers and vice versa, it's way more than just great service. Surprise isn't initiated by servants, but by leaders.

One down—let's move on. Early last spring, I unveiled my speech on Surprise as the closing keynote of a full-day symposium in front of a group of McGill University MBA students. During the seminar's lunch break, a Quantitative Methods Professor insisted that the delivering of quality is what brings about Surprise. He argued that people have been burned by shoddy workmanship and planned obsolescence for so long that when faced with quality goods and services (he used Volvo, Barney's New York, and Whole Foods as examples), they are Surprised into spending.

A valid cause-and-effect, but still not enough. After the sale of my company Airborne Mobile to the Japanese entity Cybird, I took my first trip to Tokyo, and learned firsthand about a two-tiered concept of quality I first discovered in Alex Wipperfurth's book, *Brand Hijack*. By staying in Japan's energy-efficient and "luxurious but not overboard" hotels; by taking Tokyo cabs with lace-covered seats and drivers who open doors for you from the inside; by working out in sparkling-clean gyms with fresh shorts and shirts to borrow; by being offered "umbrella condoms" to prevent my soaking wet umbrella from dripping all over myself and the store I just entered; and by being provided with form-fitting, clear plastic "bag raincoats" to protect my purchases from the inclement elements once I left, I learned the difference between the Japanese philosophies of *atarimae hinshitsu* (quality that is expected) and *mirokuteki hinshitsu* (quality that fascinates).

So quality may indeed Surprise ... but not always. The concept of quality has to rise above expectation and hover at fascination to truly do so. In other words, to best describe the relationship between the two, quality can Surprise, but it ain't Surprise.

So now we get to the big one. The "O-W" showdown. When running the original premise of this book past a former employee named Steve Hardy (known as "The Creative Generalist" throughout the blogosphere and whom I still credit for pushing me into that world), he said in his patented matter-of-fact manner: "Uh, isn't 'Surprise' just another name for 'Wow'? And doesn't Tom Peters kinda own the word Wow?"

No it's not, and no he doesn't (well, at least that's what the folks down at the United States Patent and Trademark Office assure me ... although Al Ries and Jack Trout may disagree). And even if he did, there's a big difference between the Surprise and wow. In his 1994 book *The Pursuit of Wow!* Tom frankly acknowledges that, "The best always Surprises. If Surprise = success, could we build a SURPRISE FACTORY [caps his], i.e. an organization that keeps producing Surprise?"[2] So with all due respect to Mr. Peters, one of my author idols of my college days, to put it mathematically:

Surprise >Wow

Wow can be likened to Surprise in neutral; it is potential energy being stored, waiting for its cue to become kinetic. Once put into play, Surprise trumps wow and takes it to the next level. For those not mathematically inclined, let me explain the relationship in a more visual manner.

This is wow:

!

And this is Surprise:

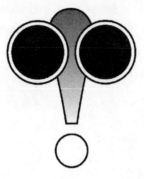

I'll admit that Tom Peters appears to have first dibs on the exclamation mark as a logo (and has used it to connote his precious and seemingly proprietary "wow"), but I've taken the piercing piece of punctuation a bit further. In the center of the Surprise pictogram (above) sits your standard exclamation point, but it is vice-gripped by two gaping circles. And, if I may be so bold in describing what has become my logo, the addition of the two circles takes the common exclamation mark and gives it the balls it needs to fully and truly Surprise.

While the circles give off strong vibes of staring down the barrel of a shotgun (quite the fitting metaphor for "Pow! Right Between the Eyes," wouldn't you say?), they are actually meant to symbolize the staring eyes themselves. Put together, the circles and punctuation mark form the semblance of a face, wide-eyed and open-mouthed ... the epitome of what we look like when we're Surprised, remember?

Here's another visual explanation. Imagine you're reading *Fortune* magazine, you turn the page and are met with the expensive, full-page ad pictured in Figure 3.1.

THE CONFERENCE BOARD

The 4th Annual

Senior Marketing Executive Roundtable

Increasing Marketing Effectiveness

April 18-19, 2007, Millennium UN Plaza, New York, NY
May 17-18, 2007, The Drake, Chicago, IL

Improve Your Top and Bottom Lines! Now!

Learn from powerhouse speakers from companies, consultancies, and universities how to increase your revenue and profits. Hear:

* What senior marketing executives say about marketing effectiveness.
* How new technologies are transforming marketing.
* How marketing metrics lead to powerful marketing and branding strategies.
* How to increase marketing ROI with profit-directed segmentation.
* How a company-wide marketing information system improves decisions.
* Which are the top 100 brands in the world and how they earned their positions.
* How to persuade senior management of the return on your branding efforts.
* How to rebuild an iconic brand.
* How to optimize your marketing communications decisions.
* Why spending more does not always mean growing more.
* How to allocate marketing resources to achieve objectives.
* How to employ a marketing mix model and determine accountability.
* How to use the marketing budget to change marketing thinking.

Join top executives from leading organizations including: Nortel, 3M, Constellation Wines, MINI, Sony, Penthouse, UPS, Yahoo!, INSEAD, Alcatel-Lucent, Hewlett-Packard, and many more.

Acquire great how-to ideas, experience vivid case histories, and learn how to increase marketing effectiveness.

This is **the marketing event** you should attend this Spring. Reserve your space now by calling our Customer Service department at (212) 339-0345 or register online at **http://www.conference-board.org/srmkg.htm**

We look forward to seeing you in New York or Chicago.

Presented with assistance from:

PROPHET

Academic Sponsor:

COLUMBIA BUSINESS SCHOOL

Media Sponsor:

BRANDWEEK

Dean Adams
Director, Corporate Brand Management
3M

Nick Besbeas
Vice President, Global Direct Marketing
Yahoo!

Kevin Clancy, Ph.D.
Chairman and Chief Executive Officer
Copernicus Marketing Consulting

Lauren Flaherty
Chief Marketing Officer
Nortel

Susan Friedman
Director of Global Events
Alcatel-Lucent

Chris Gaebler
Vice President, Corporate Marketing
Sony Electronics

James R. Gregory
Chief Executive Officer
CoreBrand

Trudy Hardy
Manager
MINI Marketing

Leslie Joseph
Vice President, Consumer Research and Consumer Affairs
Constellation Wines U.S.

Kurt Kuehn
Senior Vice President, Sales and Marketing
UPS

Jean-Claude Larreche
Alfred H. Heineken Chair of Marketing
INSEAD

Philippe Latapie
Partner and Managing Director,
StratX International

Daniel Laury
CEO
LSF Interactive

Deborah Nelson
Senior Vice President, Marketing & Alliances, Technology Solutions Group
Hewlett-Packard

Andrew Pierce
Senior Partner
Prophet

Joanna Seddon
Executive Vice President,
Millward Brown

Don Sexton
Professor of Business
Columbia University

Diane M. Silberstein
President & Publisher
Penthouse Magazine

Visit our website at http://www.conference-board.org/srmkg.htm

Figure 3.1   A jolly time for all, I'm sure.

Well, what have we here? A "Senior Marketing Executive Roundtable" where you'll learn about "Increasing Marketing Effectiveness" from "Powerhouse Speakers"! How utterly impressive! You keep reading, and two pages later, you come across another ad, also for a marketing conference, as pictured in Figure 3.2.

Figure 3.2 Post modern marketing at its best. Wish I was there.

What the hell is going on with this one? What a confusing mess! Is this some kind of mistake? Was someone's hand-drawn instruction sheet mistaken for the ad itself? Whose head will roll because of this one?

Both ads are type-driven, and are events sponsored by impeccable, corporate American stalwarts. Except for a thumbnail shot of one Scott Goodson, they are in basic black-and-white, enhanced by just one color.

Yet tell me, truthfully, which one drew your eyes, demanded your attention, piqued your curiosity? Which event will prompt passionate discussions about the **real** tomorrow of marketing?

The first conference, with an impressive C-level speaker or two, may offer some wow. The other, thumbing its nose at convention with the guts to be messy, self-parodying, and irreverent, pledges Pow!

In the speeches I give, I use these comparisons to emphasize the difference between the two.

Wow = Upgrades   *POW! = Quantum leap*

While wow may be more than incremental improvements, it still moves in steps. Surprise immediately *boings* you to new heights, to a new stratosphere, to places you never even knew existed. Wow is moving from economy to first class; Surprise teleports you miles away.

Wow = Exceed expectations   *POW! = Total shock*

In other words, wow takes you past a standard you have already set. Surprise smacks you about the head, since you never even saw it coming. Wow elicits smiles and sounds of "Hmmmm"; Surprise makes you gasp. Bill Taylor, the author of *Mavericks at Work*, clarifies the difference in a piece he wrote about the Internet shoe retailing phenomenon Zappos for the *Harvard Business Review* blog. In it, he describes the company's "free delivery, no risk, free returns anytime" business model and says:

> . . . *the value proposition is a winner. But it's the emotional connection that seals the deal. This company is fanatical about not just satisfying customers, but amazing them. The company promises free, four-day delivery. That's pretty good. But most of the time it delivers next-day, a Surprise that leaves a lasting*

impression on customers: "You said four days, but I got them the next morning.[3]

Wow = A great game   *POW! = A major upset*

Sports fans know the difference. Wow is what you talk about on the radio call-in show on the way home from the stadium. Surprise is an experience you relive over and over, share like a giant tub of popcorn, and pass along to your grandchildren. A favorite and most unlikely example was the women's college softball game last year in Oregon, when Western Oregon's tiny second baseman Sara Tucholsky hit her first-ever home run, twisted her knee while touching first base, and since being helped by a teammate or coach would wipe out her feat, was instead—in a colossal feat of sportsmanship—carried around the bases by members of the ***opposing*** team. (The story ripped around the globe like a pandemic, and was oft-discussed not just in "sport sections," but in religious circles, by ethics columnists, and among those seeking to rekindle their faith in mankind. Or in this case, womankind.)

Wow = A haircut   *POW! = A new hair color (or style)*

Wow is the way you look after coming home from your usually scheduled appointment at the hairdresser, barber, or stylist—fresh, neat, slightly different than you did before you walked in. Surprise is how you look when you decide to really go for it—not just a different look, but a different person. Don't believe me? Then try that shocking red rinse, the "fauxhawk," or the complete scalp-shave next time you're there. That's what the much-celebrated adman Alex Bogusky (of the renowned Crispin Porter & Bogusky agency) did when he was 24. "I wondered 'What kind of things did I have to do to disrupt people and make them think differently about me?'"

he told the now-defunct *Business 2.0* magazine in 2005. "I embraced this notion that every six months I would radically change my look. I did it mostly with my hair, from a crew cut to a Mohawk to long hair to a mullet. I wanted people to have to take the trouble to reanalyze what I was offering."[4]

So no, Surprise ain't wow. It's better, stronger, new, and improved. But it still ain't taken 100 percent seriously. On a societal level, Surprise has long been stuck in a no-man's land, a purgatory of poor perception. It's like the growth-spurting teenage boy at the big family wedding; loud, suitably impressive, and potent on his own, but simultaneously too sophisticated for the kids' table and not established enough to sit with the grown-ups.

I can relate. When I was running the comedy festival, I had the well-earned but unfortunate title of "CEO, Just For Laughs." It provoked a reaction, but rarely the one I wanted. The media had no problem identifying my showbiz peers at the time as CEO, HBO Films or CEO, Viacom Networks, but because of my connection to the less than Wall Street world of comedy, I was always the event's "Head Honcho" or "Boss" or "Chucklemeister"; the incongruous melange of ivory tower boardroom title and seemingly childish working environment was too much to handle at the time, I guess.

But thanks to Larry Page, Sergey Brin, Jerry Yang, and their Web 2.0 prodigy, the stigma has lessened. Nowadays, there's no shame to combine the title CEO with nonsense-sounding words like Google or Yahoo! (or other multi-million-dollar concerns with names better suited to pets such as Bebo, Squidoo, Gawker, flickr, Zappos, Plaxo, Twitter, Zillow, Joost, del.icio.us, and Digg) on your biz card. If there was any doubt that business has entered a freethinking new era, it was laid to eternal rest with this competitive comparison, written in all seriousness in *Business 2.0* magazine: "Unlike its rival Qoop, Moo can put a different image on each of the 100 MiniCards in a $20 order."[5] Today's infantesque guttural gurgling may be tomorrow's billion-dollar IPO, so cough up a few unintelligible syllables and take your stab at big business's brass ring.

Sir Richard Branson also deserves a loud shout-out for bringing together the concentric circles of silliness, significance, and Surprise. If Pow! had a poster child, it would be this bearded one. Here's a guy who plunges into a myriad of exciting but unrelated businesses in which he has no previous experience (hence the "Virgin" prefix he attaches to all of them)—a record label, a cola, an airline, a bridal shop, a railroad, a wireless carrier, a media retailer . . . over 200 companies in 30 countries. His five word due diligence process? "Screw it, let's do it."

A billionaire 7.9 times over at last count, each new business (or even new business project) that Virgin launches is marked with some sort of extreme Surprise stunt where Branson is front and center; people know he will do something, but nobody knows exactly what. He's driven a military tank down New York's Fifth Avenue, dressed up as a blushing bride, flown hot-air balloons across oceans, and jumped 75 feet from a helicopter straight down into a reception room through a small hole in a glass ceiling. Some stunts work better than others; in October of 2007 Sir Richard was blown into, and scraped down, the wall of the Las Vegas Palms' Fantasy Tower during a 407-foot plunge from its roof. All this to celebrate Virgin America's inaugural flight from San Francisco to Vegas . . . itself a journey of not much more than 407 feet. There aren't enough illicit substances in the world that I can gobble to conjure up the vision of Jack Welch, Michael

Dell, or even Larry Ellison pulling off even one of Sir Richard's exploits.

So what does all this childish adultism mean for Surprise? It means the corporate credibility breakthrough it needs is getting closer. Like we saw with the Oprah example that opened this book, Surprise can also expand the bottom line in a most delightful way. Surprise marketing isn't just for the gutter guerrillas, the street-fighters, or—as Tom Peters calls them—the "weirdoes and freaks" anymore. Slowly, surely, and surreptitiously, some serious entities are dipping their toes into the Surprise pool as well.

How much more serious can you get than America's most hallowed hall of academia, Harvard University? To promote its Harvard Business School Executive Education program in 2007, the school shocked the education establishment by using Apple-esque terms like "Break Free. Start Thinking and Acting Differently" in ads for its executive marketing management courses. The institution even went as far as altering its heralded coat of arms (see Figure 3.3) to further drive home

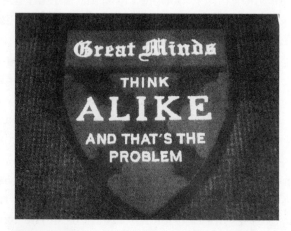

Figure 3.3

the point that this is not your great-grandfather's Harvard any-more. (If the folks at *Hah-vahd Yahd* are embracing their wild side, imagine the ramifications for the Fortune 500 in a few years.)

If a university as esteemed as Harvard can tap dance on the edges of extreme with ads like this, what's a small, lil' private school like Wilkes University in Wilkes-Barre, PA to do? Well, borrowing, but modifying, a page from Don Peppers and Martha Rogers' *The One to One Future*, Wilkes honed in on its potential student recruits with a fine-point laser beam. Every school I know claims to be focused on the individual, but for the second consecutive year, last spring Wilkes University went out and grabbed 'em by the short ones with a multimedia ad campaign that called out target candidates by name, and zoomed in on their particular achievements and passions.

For example, to attract Nicole Pollack to its freshman class, Wilkes literally made her a star, plastering her name on billboards, pizza boxes, gas pumps, and on MTV, rendering her almost as ubiquitous as Tila Tequila. Her ad read:

> *Scranton High senior Nicole Pollock: Our goal at Wilkes University is to be as much a mentor as your mother has been. (Now, if we could only make her ravioli.)*[6]

Nicole said yes, by the way. Wilkes didn't stop with her. Other ads went:

> *Hey Kristen Pecka. Only your closest friends at Central Catholic call you Pecka-lecka-lecka. Choose Wilkes University and add 2,362 more people to that list.*[7]

Or:

Liz Wendolowski. You're a star on the Meyers debate team. We hope you can settle the "ramen noodles vs. mac 'n cheese" debate at the Wilkes University dorms next year.

Each ad ended with a literal "call to action," asking the prospective (and somewhat shell-shocked, I'd imagine) candidate to "call a Colonel," the school's nickname, at 570-408-6030. The campaign cost a mere $120,000 and attracted worldwide attention worth a minimum 100 times that. The concept was conjured up by the Philadelphia-based agency 160 Over 90 (named after a high blood-pressure reading) and personifies what Darryl Cilli, the agency's executive creative director, describes as the "human reaction" that he tries to incite in consumers, a feeling you may recognize as, and hopefully now call, "Euphoric Shock." Wanna talk about Pow! Moments? Imagine driving downtown and seeing your own name calling out to you from a billboard. Try to resist a sales proposition when it comes from you.

An even tinier school, Lakehead University, also called out a candidate by name ... but his name was George W. Bush. Using the President's face as its focal point, Lakehead headlined its campaign "Yale Shmale," and drove its point home with the piledriver subhead "Graduating from an Ivy League university doesn't mean you're smart. Choosing Lakehead does." Ouch.

It's not only the institutes of higher education themselves crossing the chasm into Surpriseland; so are some of the tools they use to convey their institutionalized higher educating. In March of 2007, Stamford, Connecticut's Cengage Learning, one of the largest providers of print and digital information services for the educational and library reference markets in the world, launched a unique "learning imprint" they call 4LTR Press. The company took aim at the marketing discipline itself and trimmed down the usual cornerstone-sized (and weighted), snooze-inciting textbook into a 352-page, 8 x 10 softcover called *MKTG*, which is not just an eye-catching textbook 2.0 title but, as Cengage explained, is how students abbreviate the word in a text message and the way the course is listed in school catalogues.

More like a magazine than the backbreaking doorstoppers I had to lug around throughout college, the lean, mean *MKTG* was sold to schools and students as a "brief paperback that includes a suite of learning aids to accommodate the busy and diverse lifestyles of today's learners, like flash cards and downloads for audio, video and cell phones."[8] The 4LTR Press also backed it up with interactive games and web sites for those lucky enough to teach, and learn, from it.

The results were as inspiring as the concept itself. In its first year, the *MKTG* book was adopted by over 500 schools, which led the company to expand the 4LTR model to include books on Management (*MGMT*), Organization Behavior (*ORGB*), Economics (*ECON*), Business (*BUSN*), and Operations Management (the mantra-like *OM*).

Ironically, one of the ambassadors doing the most to bring a level of legitimacy to Surprise is a band of nomadic comedians, who are not just marketing themselves, but the clout of Surprise itself. Improv Everywhere is an—to say the very least—unorthodox comedy group who pull off nondemeaning performance art stunts they call "scenes of chaos and joy in public places," much to the amusement and confusion of everyone around them. Formed in 2001 by Charlie Todd, a member of and teacher at New York's Upright Citizen's Brigade Theater (you may remember them from their Comedy Central shows in the late 1990s), Improv Everywhere's riotous missions include:

- A fake U2 concert on a Manhattan rooftop an hour before the band's actual appearance at Madison Square Garden.

- A reading and book signing (26 copies sold!) by Anton Chekov at a well-known bookstore, despite the fact that the author had been dead for over a century.

- The setting up of three huge desktop computers and monitors at a downtown Starbucks and having people work on them as if they were laptops.

- Perhaps the pièce de résistance, the Frozen Grand Central, where 207 Improv Everywhere agents struck a still pose at Grand Central Station for five minutes, resulting in mass delightful bewilderment, a video documentation with close to 10 million views on YouTube, and a fictionalized version featuring Robin Williams on NBC's *Law & Order: SVU*.

Improv Everywhere's thinking and results embody everything one can hope for in a Surprise—brilliant planning, flawless execution, oversized impact, and the catalyst for stories that will generate Word of Mouth for years. As Todd himself has said: "My primary motive is to create moments that are so astonishing, people will have a story to tell for the rest of their lives."

What's most heartening, Surprising actually, is that Improv Everywhere is being taken very seriously by old media and new cultural institutions. The *New York Times* lauded the group's work, saying:

> *These aren't the obnoxious humiliations known to fans of MTV shows like "Punk'd" and "Boiling Points" or "Da Ali G Show" on HBO. Like a number of like-minded but unaffiliated tricksters striking elsewhere around the country, Mr. Todd and his cohorts at Improv Everywhere merely want to give people something to talk about.*

Later on in the piece, the *Times* quotes Dr. Harold Takooshian, a professor of urban psychology at Fordham University, who elevated Todd by describing his oeuvre as "breaking the unwritten laws of everyday life in the city to get people to appreciate the moment."[9] Well, there's something that'll look impressive on Charlie's resumé!

On the other end of the cool spectrum, over at the hipper-than-hip New Museum in New York's Bowery district (its four-word mission statement reads simply: "New Art, New Ideas"), Improv Everywhere was feted equally as seriously with a special event that fawned over its "unusual process, from development through execution to online promotion, including a survey of the unique problems surrounding hidden camera documentation" as well as "how the Internet is changing the way we interact with live performance and the delicate balancing act between anonymity, purity of vision, and sustainability in a world intent on coopting our imaginations in the service of any potential new marketing opportunity."[10] (Uh, David Ogilvy, you still with us?)

My mother would be proud. You don't necessarily have to talk to strangers anymore; you can just stand to the side, watching and enjoying what they do. But that's not to say you should remain silent. Great Pow! Moments often resurrect two near-obsolete expressions that were long abandoned, left to die in the crumbling archives of the archaic. These days, shouted in delight as extremes are expanded, I call them The Battle Cries of Surprise. All together now:

"What *WILL* They Think of Next?"
and
"Well, I Never!"

For the benefit of my readers of Generation Y, the former was usually uttered by up-tempo, silky-voiced narrators showing off wacky technologies like flying car prototypes in 1940s news shows, while the latter was the standard statement of Ma Kettle-ish grandmotherly types in black-and-white movies, with grey hair pulled back into a tight bun (think of Granny from the Beverly Hillbillies, or for the more cultured of you, the painting *American Gothic*), usually delivered with a hint of revulsion.

These expressions are way too relevant to remain buried in nostalgia, which is why, with you as my witness, I move to officially adopt them for the Surprise movement. "What *WILL* They Think of Next?" epitomizes that wonder and innocence of discovering something new, and glows with optimism for the future. And rid of its prudish roots, "Well, I Never!" is the culmination of great Surprise; an explosive reaction to a new idea, a new experience, a new product.

One last thing Surprise ain't—Surprise ain't tranquil. So here's to the opportunity to bellow its Battle Cries at the top of your lungs. Often—and with feeling!

Summary

STUFF YOU AIN'T GOING TO FORGET FROM CHAPTER 3

- Rife with meaning. What else is there to say?

- If Harvard University's Business School and Richard Branson can dance with Surprise, so can you. Bring comfy shoes. And Red Bull.

- Surprise is more than service, stronger than quality, and greater than wow.

- Everybody, all together now, lemme hear the Battle Cries: "What *WILL* They Think of Next?" and "Well, I Never!"

CHAPTER 4
All Powerful? Almighty? Almost.
The Surprising Surprise Conundrum

Perhaps the first three chapters raised the bar too high.

Faster than a Facebook campaign!
More powerful than a Super Bowl ad!
Able to leap customer expectations in a single bound!
Look! Up in the sky! It's a *Surprise*!

By now, you should be all hopped up on the potential and the potency of the **Pow!** Moment. You can't help but be impressed with the influence of Surprise: it commands clout, has extensive reach, and performs amazing feats of strength. My God, is there anything it *can't* do? Never mind its status as "Marketing's Secret Weapon," Surprise seems to be nothing short of the genre's Superman.

Well that's a complimentary comparison, but even Superman, with his all-embracing powers, isn't completely invulnerable. The one major chink in his armor is that glowing green rock called Kryptonite. Just its simple proximity weakens him severely. Brings him to his knees.

It's the same with Surprise. While it thankfully handles rocks (of all colors) with great ease, its singular Achilles heel can render it ineffective and impotent. Ironically, the main weakness of Surprise is Surprise itself. Like the ravenous snake that eats its own tail, the success of any one Surprise is the starting point for its eventual demise.

Here's why: in today's rapidly shrinking and hyper-connected world, words travel fast—really, really fast. So the eye-popping extremes that are spawned by Surprise soon turn into eye-rubbing standards (also really, really fast). Yes, people are still juiced by extremes, but unfortunately, for nowhere near as long as they once were.

These days, product life cycles are rapidly abbreviated. New goods and services go from "hot and hip" to "ho-hum" in record time. It used to be that a company would enjoy a nice bit of breathing room after introducing something new and noteworthy. The buzz generated by the innovation, the soil shifted by its groundbreaking nature, would engrave the company in consumer hearts and minds for years to come. But no more.

Think about Chrysler's PT Cruiser. Launched to great fanfare in April 2000, the striking retro design immediately became the rage of the road. People pointed at 'em, oohed-and-ahhed as they drove by. There were waiting lists of nearly a year, which led to some of the cars being sold for twice their suggested list price. A year later, the PT Cruiser surprised everyone when it was named the North American Car of the Year; making the 2001 Top Ten list of the prestigious *Car and Driver* magazine further enhanced its popularity and mystique.

Break out the champagne! But uh, don't open it just yet. Before long, Cruiser overkill crept in. What was once the coolest of cool rides soon became something kind of embarrassing to be seen driving. In December 2007, just eight model years after its most auspicious debut, the PT Cruiser was discontinued. An abrupt and ice-cold ending for a one-time white-hot hit.

Tales like this are now becoming the norm, not the exception. Consider the ABC primetime TV quiz show *Who Wants to Be a Millionaire?* It first hit the American airwaves in 1999 and went from being an unavoidable cultural craze, to an over-wrought cliché, to being canceled by the network in a period of just three years. (Today, it exists only on the slushpile of daytime syndication. Check your local listings.)

Then there are the mega-hyped lotteries like Power-ball and Megamillions, who have had to up their antes exponentially to combat a phenomenon lottery officials call "Jackpot Fatigue." This can't be blamed on monetary deval-uation; it's yet another example of expectation inflation. As Jennifer Lee details in her book, *The Fortune Cookie Chronicles,*

> ... *today's players needed ever-larger jackpots to entice them into buying tickets. The threshold for an attention-grabbing megajackpot had once been $10 million; (in 2005) it now stood at $100 million.*[1]

Add about 473 different brands of me-too energy drinks to the list (Gatorade and Red Bull, what hath you wrought?). Throw another blade on that Gillette razor. Knock out another Crocs knock-off. Even the holy grail of hip consumer products, Apple's cherished iPod, has fallen victim to this ho-hum ennui. Now I love the iPod, but practically every flashing banner ad on the web is giving one away if you "click here now." Banks across the nation are offering them as the bonus if you open a new account. They're a door prize

at every raffle, charity event, and tradeshow booth. The eyes
are so *off* this prize. One nation underwhelmed.

Don't blame the consumer for being excessively fickle.
Rabid competition leads to rapid indifference. As *Time*
magazine's James Poniewozik puts it: "Nothing is more shim-
meringly beautiful than the next big thing in our imagination;
nothing is sadder than the next big thing become reality."[2]
Right before our eyes, today's notion of "new" hastily deteri-
orates into "nu?" (a very efficient Yiddish term that roughly
translates to "so, already?"). Miss the first wave of excitement,
no big deal; there's another coming at you before you know
it. The fast-forward-thinking Japanese mobile operator NTT
DoCoMo succinctly and elegantly summarized the situation
in one of its trade ads with this slogan:

SO RADICAL TODAY, SO OBVIOUS TOMORROW.

So therein lies Surprise's "Elephant in the Room" problem,
the conundrum that must be confronted: Surprise is fleeting.
Any one Surprise doesn't last; no matter how loud the Pow!—
its effect is ephemeral. To truly pay dividends, Surprise must
thrive as a continuum. That's why instead of being creative
once, true Surprise requires "shocking the system," and finding new extremes on a constant basis. The driving factor of
successful Surprise is a flow, not the spectacular one-off.

Remember my definition from Chapter 2? If not, don't
turn back, here it is again:

**Surprise: The constant expansion
of the boundaries of delightful extremes**.

While it probably flew under your radar screen back then,
the most important word in this definition is "constant." Surprise isn't just a shock, it's an addiction to them. As a concept,
it keeps on demanding. But the rewards are well worth the
effort.

Why do you think people keep returning to Costco to shop (and pay membership fees for the privilege of doing so) week after week? The prices? Indeed, they help, but I can name you a dozen other retail chains that also offer low, low prices.

The reason Costco customers continue to thunder in as a herd is for the unexpected. While the stores themselves may look like dull, giant grey warehouses from the outside, when it comes to Surprise, they drastically out-shock any ritzy Fifth Avenue designer boutique. Surprise isn't just a strategy at Costco; it's the corporation's core DNA. This was illuminated by Matthew Boyle in a piece he wrote on the company for *Fortune* magazine in which he said:

> *Costco's card-carrying legions come in droves, waiting anxiously in fancy foreign cars on Saturday mornings for the store to open. Carts in hand, they display a fervor not usually seen outside of houses of worship. While Wal-Mart stands for low prices, and Target embodies cheap chic, Costco is a retail treasure hunt.*[3]

A treasure hunt! Can it be described any better, any more electric than that? Think about it—a different experience, new excitement every time you're at the store. No wonder Costco is second only to Best Buy in annual retail sales per square foot.

And Costco unburies its treasure day after day after day, exemplifying the all-important flow of which I preach. Along with cases of ketchup and mayonnaise and paper towels and printer ink and other staples, Costco continues to serve up new, disparate stuff at wild prices. A recent check of its web site shows a product mix ranging from a $4,000 massage chair to a three-person sauna to Calvin Klein's Euphoria men's cologne to hockey cards to the world's best kosher hot dogs.

Compare this to the ultimate retail cliché (and one that sadly sullies the subject matter of this book): the Surprise Sale . . . which is usually neither much of a Surprise nor a sale.

Despite the huge headline and the classic wide-eyed, open-mouthed Surprise faces that trumpet them (see Figures 4.1 and 4.2), there's rarely anything to get excited about.

Figure 4.1   Don't get so excited . . .

Figure 4.2 ... but nothing else, unfortunately.

Frankly, the only thing Surprising about these sales is that after years of all promise and no delivery, people actually believe that there is some sort of shock waiting for them inside the pages of flyers like the ones that lurk behind Figures 4.1 and 4.2.

Inside, for those gullible enough to actually take a look in the belief that something will be truly worthy of the eye-popping expression, is nothing more than the same ol' song and dance, like:

- Don't pay until whenever

- Some sort of percentage-off

🍄 An insignificant gift with purchase of something

🍄 Run-of-the-mill merchandise in familiar settings

Too much copy, not nearly enough reason to read it. Bad enough on its own, but worse still when packaged with a promise of Surprise. A double whammy: boring **and** misleading.

Don't let the name fool you—these sales don't sustain constant Surprise. They merely repeat the word. Repetition is good if you're a parrot, but not if you want to create ongoing marketing Surprise. In his book *Brand: It Ain't the Logo (It's What People Think of You)*, Ted Matthews lays out the challenge this way:

> *Coming up with something "fresh" (like Burnett has continually done for the Maytag Man) is actually a lot harder than dreaming up something "new." New means the freedom to start over on a clean canvas every time. Being fresh requires that you always work in a single, unchanging context: what the brand actually stands for.*[4]

Yup, the task of sustaining constant Surprise in business is arduous, stressful, and challenging. But don't worry if you're not up for it. I'm sure some of your competition will be.

Whoa . . . them's fighting words. It's time to get you prepped for the battle ahead.Surprise—like anything else majestic, rare, and delicious—is a perishable good, a rapidly perishable one at that. An old Surprise is like a rotten peach. At one time it was gorgeous, fresh, tasty, and good. Past its expiration date, it's just yuck.

A perfect example is explained by this musical interlude: many moons ago, 1974 to be exact, singer/songwriter Jim Stafford had a huge Surprise hit with a little ditty entitled My Girl Bill. "Holy jumpin' Jeez," was North America's initial reaction to the song, "this guy's singing about his girlfriend, who's name is Bill!" (Remember, this was the early 1970s, when this was somewhat more shocking than it is in these enlightened times . . .)

Sung by the very male Stafford, the tune starts by describing how a fellow named Bill walks him to his door and challenges him about the odd nature of this love affair they appear to share. To avoid the gossip of nosy neighbors, Stafford quickly invites Bill inside, and offers to fix him a drink. (Imagine, all that steamy innuendo, and we're still in the first verse!) The song continues with its chorus, where Stafford pledges love and affection for his "girl Bill."

Still with me? Take a whiff of smelling salts, haul yourself off the floor and let's continue. The song pulls you deeper into its homoerotic vortex as the pair share wine, lock eyes, and try to understand the nature of their confused love. And at the very moment when you are unsure whether to call your congressman or take a cold shower, the song lurches into its shocking, twisted climax where Stafford reveals that both he and Bill just love the same female, and then tells his wine-sipping rival to take a hike, because "She's my girl . . . Bill!"

The last line of the song mercifully pays off its lame-o joke, and thankfully restored a sense of decency to the nation back in 1974. No, Stafford wasn't singing about "My Girl Bill," he was singing about "My Girl . . . Bill" (note the placement of the punctuation; he was talking to his buddy Bill about his girl). I know, I know, you're just about splitting your sides right now. Pull yourself together for the point of all this:

☂ The first time you heard "My Girl Bill" on the radio, you were taken aback.

☂ The second time, you watched to see if anyone you were with didn't know the Surprise ending, and waited to enjoy their reaction.

☂ The third time, you wanted to shoot the radio.

☂ The fourth time, you wanted to shoot Jim Stafford.

☂ The fifth time, you wanted to shoot yourself.

See what I mean by "perishable good"? This is why magicians never "do it again." When I was a teenager, I made some extra money performing magic at kids' birthday parties. With every great effect—rocks transformed into candy, coins appearing from midair, small animals disappearing— the squealed refrain from the pipsqueak audience was, "Do it again!" But you couldn't; the kids would know what to look for, the delight would be lost, and one smart-ass punk would inevitably bark, "I know how he does it!" (And once that chasm is crossed, the thrill is really gone. In fact, that's why I gave up the hobby. Once I knew how each trick was done, its appeal withered to me, no matter how much it fooled my audience.)

Expecting a Surprise just serves to accelerate its deterioration process. Now you understand the motives of comedian Sacha Baron Cohen, who had to retire his Borat character after the monumental success of the film, *Borat: Cultural Learnings of America for Make Benefit Glorious Nation of Kazakhstan*. As an unknown, he could get away with just about anything. But as an instantly recognizable icon of stupidity, people were in on the joke. His power to get people to lay down their guards and say or do shocking things was neutered. Put another way, director Alfred Hitchcock, the master of suspense, once said, "There's no terror in a bang, only in the anticipation of it."

With Surprise though, things work in exactly the opposite way: the excitement is the Surprise, not the anticipation of it. That's a lesson that one of Hitchcock's contemporaries, director M. Night Shyamalan, could've benefited from. Take a look at the box office takes of his film career:

1999	*The Sixth Sense*	$293,506,292
2000	*Unbreakable*	$95,011,339
2002	*Signs*	$227,966,634
2004	*The Village*	$114,197,520
2006	*Lady in the Water*	$42,285,169
2008	*The Happening*	$63,818,579

See the pattern? While *Signs* bumped up the numbers after *Unbreakable* (no doubt with help from superstar name Mel Gibson), Shyamalan's trend bends markedly downward after his breakthrough "I see dead people" debut with *The Sixth Sense*. It's easy to understand why. Moviegoers essentially knew what was going to happen at every one of his movies; they were going to sit through 90 minutes of story that would eventually veer wildly off the rails with a twisted "gotcha!" closing scene.

In doing this, Shyamalan committed a cardinal sin—he made the element of Surprise predictable and boring. It's as if the kids at my magic shows finally got their wish—

Shyamalan succumbed and did it again. And the public was lying in wait for it—but fewer of them each successive time. Worse yet were the critics, who were also waiting, but with howitzer blasts like this aimed at his most recent oeuvre, *The Happening:*

- "The final explanation, which comes as no surprise, is more preposterous than profound." *—The New York Daily News*

- "Shyamalan's such an eager recycler, grinding out the same ideas and images again and again. The man who showed such promise less than a decade ago has been leaving a diminishing creative footprint ever since." *—Salon.com*

- "No one will watch any of Shyamalan's recent films twice. [*The Happening*] can barely be watched once." *—New York Post*

- "It's downright stupid." *—Detroit News*

In spite of these attacks, I think Shyamalan is a gifted writer and director, but if he really wants to shock us now, his next film should have no Surprise ending at all. Or be an animated film. Or a small art film. Or whatever. As long as he breaks his pattern. That is, if Hollywood ever again trusts him with the keys to the car.

Eagle-eyed cynics among you may be saying: "Hold on a minute, how can you criticize poor M. Night? He practiced exactly what you preached! He created Surprise on a constant basis!"

Well, not exactly. There's a monumental difference between conjuring up consistent Surprise and recycling the same one over and over. This is something I learned from none other than Donald Trump (uh, sort of).

In the early days of my mobile media company, when it was called Airborne Entertainment, our marketing budget was miniscule, and spent primarily for making a splash at the semiannual Cellular Telecommunications Industry Association (CTIA) Conference. At CTIAs past, to keep Airborne face-forward, we would produce some sort of take-away collateral or swag, each of which would cost us about five or six bucks.

Unfortunately, the ROI on these standard items (t-shirts, glossy brochures, bouncy balls, the usual suspects) was less than spectacular, and at the San Francisco conference in spring of 2004, we were looking to spend less but get more bang for the buck, particularly since we were launching our mobile version of Donald Trump's *Real-Estate Tycoon* game at the time.

Our brainstorm process went from "What can we do *for* a buck?" to "What can we do *with* a buck?" The end result, captured by the photos shown in Figures 4.3 and 4.4, reduced our per-unit cost to about $1.02.

Figure 4.3   Can I really go to jail for this?

Figure 4.4   Still the greatest bang for the buck I've ever seen.

This was no photocopy or flimsy replica of legal tender; we took 1,000 actual singles and painstakingly rubber-stamped them with a pertinent promotional message, which led interested parties to our show booth and a special website.

People were more than interested. They flipped out. First, they flipped at Airborne. "Are you crazy? We can't screw around with the U.S. Mint!" the staff panicked. "Won't we get arrested for that?"

"I hope so," I replied. "Just think of all the publicity!"

(Truth be told, we used a vegetable-based ink that would fade over time . . . hopefully before I'd get out of prison for defacing American currency.)

Then, they flipped at CTIA. On day one of the event, we sprinkled the money on the conference floor and had a blast watching different reactions to the free dollar bills. Some people discreetly picked 'em up and pocketed 'em; some looked both ways for hidden cameras before stooping; some grabbed, read, and laughed; some ignored them completely, adhering to the "If It's Too Good To Be True . . ." theorem.

A pleasant buzz was building, but no big bang—yet. The flare-up I'd been looking for came the following afternoon, when I was speaking on a panel about mobile games. The ballroom was packed for two reasons—the subject matter was important for the fledgling industry, and one of the panelists was the neoceleb Trip Hawkins, a cofounder of gaming giant Electronic Arts. Airborne, as a small company punching above its weight at the time, had to make a splash here. And I had 700 or so single friends left to help.

At one point in the panel, as per the agenda, we were supposed to talk about our most recent project. The countdown began. As I started my shpiel, I surveyed the crowd. Seated in the corners of the room were four Airborne coconspirators, each with $150 of the Trump bills in their hands; I had the other $100. The plan was as soon as I finished the sentence ". . . but we decided to promote this the Donald's way!" we would toss the bills high into the air as a catalyst to reactions unknown.

And toss we did. From my vantage point on the dais, it was a thing of beauty. Poof! Five little clouds of cash, each rising up like firework explosions before cascading to earth like giant snowflakes. And then the real explosion began— bedlam!

The gathered crowd bolted from their chairs and battled for fistfuls of dollars. Chairs flew, bodies dove, tables overturned. Decorum was shattered into dust. Hawkins was incredulous. "How do I follow that?" he moaned out loud into his mic.

Once the bills had been scooped up and the combatants returned to their seats, the panel went on, but the "damage" was done. The room was vibrating, people were chattering, and there was little attention paid to anything else than what had just happened. Conference organizers even went as far as suggesting I be banned from further events because Airborne had "upstaged their paying sponsors."

Needless to say, the stunt was the talk of the rather staid conference. Here are two of the "reviews" from influential industry bloggers:

> *Over at the Moscone West Center it was down to Airborne's Andy Nulman to liven up the definitive panel on mobile entertainment. It's been a long time since I've seen a panel member throw dollar bills to the audience.*
>
> **—Monty's Gaming and Wireless Outlook**

> *In one memorable moment, Andy Nulman flung about 100 singles in the air. Although each of these had an advertisement for the company's Donald Trump's Real Estate Tycoon printed on it, they were much sought after by a suddenly enlivened crowd. Several dozen mobile executives scrambling in response to Nulman's extension of largesse seemed an appropriate metaphor.*
>
> **—Gamespot**[5]

For the next two days, I couldn't take two steps without someone asking, "Are you the guy who threw the money?" or, more often, asking for a sample.

And to this day, eight full CTIAs later, people still come up to me and inquire: "Are you throwing any more dollar bills this time?" Of course not. That's exactly what they'd be expecting. Been there, done that . . . and unlike M. Night Shyamalan, I won't do it again. To be true to my school, I've got to find new ways to Surprise.

Subsequent Airborne CTIA Pow! moments featured *Maxim* girls bringing pedestrian traffic to a standstill by sitting smack-dab in the middle of Atlanta's Convention Center floor handing out freshly kissed copies of the magazine, a flying 15-foot tall Stewie Griffin inflatable to celebrate our deal with Fox's *Family Guy* in New Orleans, and a party that culminated in an R-rated male-female game of Twister in Las Vegas. And in the year when we decided to stop everything and do nothing, people assumed we were putting on an event so secret and exclusive, they begged us for invitations.

Let me tell you, there were times at Airborne when my staff and I spent late nights tearing our hair out, barking, and throwing things at each other trying to come up with new, never-before-seen techniques to excite, attract, and delight. We could've thrown in the towel, taken the easy way out, and recycled the dollar bill idea. But we didn't. And in the end, each time, we were proud that we hung in there and kept challenging ourselves to Surprise.

If you think this one-upping one's self sounds a bit like a game, you're not far off. In *Get Back in the Box*, Douglas Rushkoff's excellent book on innovation, he cites the work of scholar James P. Carse, most notably his manifesto entitled, *Finite and Infinite Games*.

"Finite play, like that of a kid playing a video game by the rules, ends when a winner is declared," Rushkoff explains. "Rules are fixed, and the 'element of Surprise' is used only to defeat one's foes. Infinite play, on the other hand, like that of a fantasy role-player, is never supposed to end. The only real object is to keep the game going. Instead of using Surprise to vanquish one's opponents, Surprise becomes a way to sustain everyone's interest in what's happening."

Rushkoff goes on to quote Carse, who doesn't just validate Surprise, but lays down a less-than-subtle Armageddon-like warning: "Infinite players play in the expectation of being Surprised. If Surprise is no longer possible, all play ceases."[6]

In the game of business, as in the game of life or the games of video, the two most dreaded words are "Game Over." So in giving credence to Carse's claim, it appears that the persistent quest for the new, fresh, and eye-popping is not just a simple challenge or a "put another notch in my belt" ego-boost. It's a modern-day necessity that spreads its wings much wider than the discipline of consumer marketing. In his book *Stumbling Upon Happiness*, Harvard psychology professor Daniel Gilbert explains (albeit tongue-in-cheek):

> *Among life's cruelest truths is this one: Wonderful things are especially wonderful the first time they happen, but their wonderfulness wanes with repetition. Psychologists call this habituation, economists call this declining marginal utility ... and the rest of us call it marriage.*[7]

The most successful marketers know that it's never "just business." The foundation of all marketing is the relationship between seller and buyer, and Surprise is a key element to a long-lasting one, no matter what type of relationship we're talking about. Think back to your first date with your current, or most recent, significant other. Whether it was love at first sight or the proverbial Date From Hell, what mattered most, and stayed with you longest, were the things that Surprised you.

Here's the situation: two relative strangers come together in an effort to potentially become one. For this random pairing to have even the slightest hope of ever bonding, the interested parties need to establish some common ground. So, as an opening thrust-and-parry, they each toss out a few factoids, hoping to initiate a positive connective reaction.

And the positive reactions that really magnetize are the ones that raise the eyebrows, the "I didn't knows." Things like, "I didn't know you were into Tom Waits!" or "I didn't know you were so environmentally conscious!" or "I didn't know you also had a parent die of cancer." These are more than simple statements, they are openings inviting one to go further, to explore deeper. They are Velcro hooks in search of loops to latch onto. (Why do you think I started off this book with the multiple revelations of **"The 10 Rather Surprising Things You Should Know About Me"**? It was no measly ego trip. I was looking to establish a link, a common ground with *YOU* even before you got to the prologue! So tell me, did it work?)

I don't want to get all Dr. Phil on you here, but I believe that the diminishing element of Surprise over the years is why so many personal relationships break down. As per Daniel Gilbert, "Wonderfulness wanes with repetition." Among even the most wildly wonderful couples, after a while, every story has been told dozens of times, just about every action is expected, and every move seems to be choreographed. The Surprise "I Didn't Knows" that once enthralled shrivel up and dwindle into a numbing routine of "I Know, I Know, I Knows"... a spirit cynically but hilariously captured by Stephan Pastis in the Sunday panel of *Pearls Before Swine*, reproduced here in Figure 4.5.

Boredom kills all types of relationships. Predictability doesn't just breed contempt, it has become the lucrative lifeblood of divorce lawyers everywhere (as well as of bankruptcy trustees, as businesses stultify and crumble).

Figure 4.5

So ... back to the conundrum, which just got substantially tougher. If indeed everything new is in fact old again, if extremes do turn standard really fast, if one isn't good enough and you need a flow, how on earth can Surprise survive?

It does thanks to a condition called The Surprise Half-Life. On the surface, Surprise appears to be a one-way ticket to happiness. Once you arrive at your destination, there's no return. Like in "My Girl Bill," once delivered, the original effect is then rendered ineffective. After spreading its joy, the Surprise has been depleted for you.

Yet here's the big "But": It may be over for you directly, *but* a Surprise can bring you an almost equal amount of pleasure indirectly by turning someone else onto it. In fact, great Surprises *expect* you to pass them along, as stories you just *need* to tell others. This is the fundamental first step in healing the Achilles heel.

Like a ghost, the spirit of Surprise lives on long after the original has ceased to be. This is why I've said throughout this book that the element of Surprise is the spark that ignites the increasingly influential inferno of Word of Mouth marketing. Great Surprises generate great tales; long-lasting legends.

But more than a mere collection of stories, great Surprises provide us with something more substantial, something I call The Highlight Reel of Life. Think about this for a minute. Think back to the great Surprise moments in your life, the highlights you *still* talk about. Not just the bargains or exquisite service, but the unexpected visit from an overseas friend, the Surprise birthday party for your twenty-ninth, the time your prejob interview haircut morphed into a high-flying Afro perm, the crisp $100 bill you found in the secondhand coat you bought for five bucks, the time your favorite band reached into the audience and brought you up on stage to sing . . .

I could go on forever. Hopefully, so can you. This Highlight Reel is life without the drudgery, steak without the fat, sandwiches without the crust, the ends without the means. The lows and the in-betweens have all been eliminated, leaving only the highs. This is not just the stuff you want to remember, it's the stuff you want everybody else to know.

As David Mamet (the Pulitzer Prize-winning playwright of ear-ringers like *Glengarry Glen Ross* and *Speed-the-Plow*) said in his book *The Wicked Son*, "Each human being has a certain amount of awe that must be discharged."[8]

And as unhygienic as this may sound, your discharge of awe is somebody else's influx of same. The Surprise Half-Life spreads like the proverbial virus, inspires others, and gives you increased impetus to come up with more things to talk about.

Given the influence of the Surprise Half-Life, perhaps the aforementioned ravenous snake really isn't eating its own tail. Look closely; it's just grabbing onto it so it can become a circle. A virtuous one. A reel, on which to spool, store, show, and share life's high points.

Keeping that Highlight Reel spinning should facilitate the quest to once and for all conquer the conundrum. In theory, the answer is so simple: "Don't Just Surprise, Keep Surprising." In practice though, it's somewhat more daunting. It's like saying "It's easy to get rich. Just make more money." Generating Surprise may only take a few hours to learn, but it takes years to master.

So forget the one-trick pony of "My Girl Bill" (and shed no tears for Jim Stafford, who remains to this day one of the biggest stars in the tourist wonderland of Branson, Missouri).

The *true* theme song of constant Surprise is one sung by Bonnie Raitt: "Let's Give 'Em Something to Talk About."

In the next chapter, we'll discover the most important ingredient in learning to do so.

Summary

Four Powerful Points from Chapter 4

- Don't get too giddy, Surprise is not invulnerable. Worse yet, its main weakness is itself.

- One Surprise is not enough; for it to be truly effective, Surprise must be a constant flow. Surprise is not a shock, but an addiction.

- The truth about Surprise Sales—most of them ain't.

- Consider Surprise a rapidly perishable good that must be replenished quickly. Expecting a Surprise only serves to accelerate this deterioration process. Maintaining the flow ensures that it never comes.

CHAPTER 5

Shock 101

Welcome to Surprise U, also known around pedagogical circles as the Institute of Higher Expectations. Before we even dare to delve into our curriculum, we wouldn't have any cred as a Surprise Marketing learning center if we accepted you into the program without the essential prerequisites.

Well, let's narrow that down to the singular, as there's only one true prerequisite at Surprise U: The Willingness to Stand Out.

Or, put another way:

THE WILLINGNESS
TO
STAND OUT, BABY!

The shy need not apply. Join your local convent instead. And now, please put your hands together for a brief word from our esteemed Admissions Officer, faculty member Garry Kasparov. Over to you, comrade:

"Ultimately, what separates a winner from a loser is the willingness to do the unthinkable. Intelligence without audaciousness is not enough."[1]

This from a Grandmaster of chess, of all things! (Imagine how outlandish he would be if he were a NASCAR driver or a WWE wrestler.)

Garry's point is blunt: if you're not willing to be bombastically fantastic, to howl among a world of whisperers, to be the glowing neon in a palette of flat black and white, you might as well close this book right now. Truth be told, I'm astonished that you actually got this far into it.

I can't overemphasize the critical nature of this first step . . . so I'll let the most authoritative Peter Georgescu, the chairman emeritus and former CEO of Young & Rubicam, do it for me:

Commodization—what I see as the cancer of 21st century commerce—has fueled ferocious price competition, leading to lower prices, margins and profits for businesses. With price as the only real differentiator, producers are left with a challenge: They must find a way to stand out in the crowd.[2]

Standing out is both a mindset and a lifestyle, a perpetual cause-and-effect relationship for breeding Surprise, where one feeds off the other. To best understand the Standing Out mindset, let me take you inside . . . and underground—literally.

I learned the value of this subterranean headspace four years ago, when I was invited to speak at my college alma mater during its annual "Management Career Day." I expected to be feted in the school's mahogany-paneled Executive Lounge on the sixth floor, or in the theater-grade main auditorium on the entrance level—foolish me. I must admit to being a little bummed when I discovered that my talk was sequestered in the absolute last room in the building, a windowless box tucked into a faraway corner in the school's almost forgotten basement.

But after cautiously entering the class, I found it filled with motivated, interesting, and interested students, and realized that I had actually lucked out big time. We enjoyed a rollicking, no holds barred, reality-spoken-here session for the scheduled 90 minutes, after which neither I nor the students wanted to leave, so we extended our time together for another 30 ... and then some of the keener ones invited me to the cafeteria for coffee. Meanwhile, up in the auditorium, a packed room fell asleep listening to a grey-suited captain of industry drone on and on and on with his P.R. firm-approved notes and generic PowerPoint slides.

The basement may not be as luxurious or initially desirable as other aboveground rooms, but it's where "the cool kids" hang out. It's where you'll find the secret labs and the buried treasure. It's where the exciting, close-to-the-edge stuff we all love is born. It's where Bob Dylan and the Band recorded *The Basement Tapes*, which John Rockwell of the *New York Times* called, "The greatest album in the history of American popular music."[3] When I was a kid in my parents' house, they forfeited the use of the basement and allowed me to take the whole thing over as my room. It was crammed with posters, albums, music and sports memorabilia, and all sorts of other junk. More importantly, it was where I was able to be me, without pretense, without pressure, and without judgment.

Although the basement may at times appear vacant and barren, you're never alone for long when down there. You'll be amazed at the amount, and the type, of people who share your vision, your guts, and your space. People like Robert Erlich, the head and namesake of "Robert's American Gourmet," a $50 million snack food brand that's been described as having "no artificial ingredients, no formal marketing, and no apologies." The company's trendy signature product, "Pirate's Booty" cheese puffs, was spawned when Robert picked up misshapen scrap leftovers of an aborted puff production run on a factory floor, and decided that these twisted orphans would fill his bags instead of the perfectly-formed ones the supplier was pitching. "I'm always looking through the garbage," he admits candidly, "because the mistakes are the stuff other people don't want, but I do." Some of his other obtuse product names include Caviar Potato Flyers, Stem Cell Chips, and Bubble Tea Popcorn. "I don't do anything normal," says Robert. "You're not going to see a sour cream and onion chip from me."[4]

You may also run into Phillippe Starck, the French rebel designer of ghost chairs, spider-shaped juicers, organic food, and hotels. Given his "renaissance man" heritage, he can call himself anything he wants, but chooses "a producer of Surprise" as his descriptive title. His somewhat subversive formula for creativity? "Be free. Don't care about anything, and never listen to anybody."[5]

Then there's Gary Veynerchuk. This guy makes a basement look like a penthouse. You won't have to look hard
to find him; he's brash with a cymbal clash. He took his
family's New Jersey liquor store (with $6 million in sales),
transformed it into "The Wine Library" ($50 million in
sales), and then established himself as a Web 2.0 celeb
with Wine Library TV, a video blog now known as "The
Thunder Show" that pulls in tens of thousands of views
every day. He did such a bang-up job branding himself
and his business that he became a branding consultant
(or as he puts it, a "social media sommelier") himself,
and boasts on his eponymous website that he "is willing
to go to the mat and work to make things happen for
anyone who really *Brings the Thunder*."[6]

No, that's not an earthquake you feel rumbling below
your feet; it's Robert and Phillipe and Gary and their
basement-dwelling brethren and sistren conjuring up
their next acts. So, step 1-A in setting yourself up to sys-
tematically spawn Surprise is to get your mind out of the
gutter and install it someplace even deeper. Think like a
mad scientist. Hunker down in your brain's bunker. Dare
to mess. Don't worry about the chaos or disorder. Take
the necessary plunge into life's basements.

But don't stay there for long. Step 1-B is the Surprise
Lifestyle you've got to live once you come up for sunlight
and air. And glory. And profit. Let's face it, "Generating
Surprise" is only a tactic. It's an incredibly effective one,
the inspiration for this book, but it's a tactic that belongs
to the greater strategy of "Attracting Attention." And as
we learned in Chapter 3, that's a key strategy to survive

in today's hyper-competitive world. Other than the CIA, I don't care what business you are in—going unnoticed is a one-way ride on the highway to going broke.

To that end, while writing parts of this book at an outdoor café, I took note of two older gentlemen sitting at tables near me. One guy wore a shapeless pair of beige khakis, an off-white, long-sleeved polo shirt, and a beat-up pair of what I think were once Hush Puppies. The other wore a sky blue sport jacket, red flower in his lapel, and an aqua blue cap. He had a wide white mustache and an even wider white smile. So tell me, who do you think attracted more eyeballs? Who would you think has better tales to tell? More importantly, who would you rather hang out with? Better still, if you had to choose, which one of them would you rather *be*?

I'll give you another, purely personal, example. It's about the car I drive on warm, sunny days—my beloved 1960 Corvette convertible. People who know me can't believe I can be so attached to a piece of metal (well, fiberglass in my case), because I am not one of those obsessive creatures known as a "car guy." I'm an aesthetic guy, and a guy who uses aesthetics to stand out and Surprise. Yet that's what makes my convertible such a great companion. That's it in Figure 5.1, with my son Hayes at the helm.

My office's garage is cut deep underground (easy access to my own secret lab, of course), with a dangerously steep driveway that peaks and spills onto a bar-and-restaurant-filled pedestrian mall called Prince Arthur Street. I actually have two cars, a black Jaguar X-Type and the aforementioned Vette. When I roar up

Figure 5.1 My son Hayes in the classic 1960 Corvette at the drive-in.

the driveway in the Jag, nobody gives me a second look (unless I almost run someone over at the top). I am anonymous—Mr. Cellophane.

But when I do the same in the Vette, all action on the street freezes as if I had driven into the middle of another Improv Everywhere stunt. The car is a retina-magnet, a conversation starter, a target for pointed fingers. People instinctively gather around, start to chat, and for some strange reason, give me the thumbs-up sign. The Corvette hoopla adds at least five minutes to the journey every time I leave work in it.

You see, the Vette is more than a mere automobile. I know it sounds trite, but it's a Magic Car (Really—no hype). No matter where I go with it, it brightens people's moods. It inspires upbeatness. Everyone smiles.

Ev-er-y-one: from burly, menacing Hell's Angels to curious Chassidic Rabbis. From little old ladies to major babes. From gearheads to eggheads. From nobodies to superstars (at the premiere party for his film *The Deal*, actor William H. Macy hung outside to talk about the car for 10 minutes before walking the red carpet in). Kids ask to pose for pictures with it ("It's a superhero car!" one Brazilian boy cried), and producers have asked to use it in movies ("Sure ... as long as you cast me with it," I tell them). Valet parkers leave it as a beacon in front of the entrances to their restaurants and hotels. If I had a dollar for every time someone asked to buy it, I myself could buy two more of them. No matter where I go, people stop me, roll down their windows, shout from balconies and ask me the same three questions:

"What year is it?"   (Answer: 1960)

"How big is the engine?"   (Answer: No clue ... whatever you say)

"Is it the original paint?"   (This one kills me .... I just say "Yeah")

What's more, the Vette inspires no envy. People tend to adopt it and treat it like it's their own. Once, outside a restaurant, my son Hayes and I watched as some guy admired the car, then reached inside to pick out some of the early autumn leaves that had fallen on my seats. Another time, outside a chi-chi designer's boutique, a girl ripped into a slickster who just so happened to park his Ferrari behind my car. "If you wanna impress someone, park behind a Chrysler minivan," she screamed for some bizarre reason. "This car beats your car's ass!" Thank God he didn't beat hers ... or mine.

What's even more impressive is that this car is close to a half-century old. Most people on the cusp of 50 are starting to slow down, to gravitate toward beige and boring. The Vette shows that, like my sartorially-splendored homie at the café, audacious old guys can still cut it.

Audacious and classic yes, but equally as important, the Vette is uncomplicated. There's no correlation between intricacy and interest. As hot as this car is, it's a simple piece of work deep down. No power anything. Roll-down windows that don't roll down all the way. Steering that's a better workout than my gym regimen. All powered by an engine, that while big and roaring, is positively Flinstonian compared to its modern-day brethren. Still, the Vette turns heads whiplash fast—Everywhere, every time. Such is the power of drawing attention, of Standing Out.

The upshot of all this attention is even more powerful—a shower of admiration, not one of resentment or ridicule, which are the two greatest fears, and thus impediments, of trying to stand out in the first place. Rhonda Byrne made a fortune with her compilation book

The Secret, which she says "reveals the most powerful law in the universe ... the Law of Attraction." (I think the *real* Secret is getting a whole bunch of other people to write your book for you, but I digress.) But as much as you may sit in hope and wait for it, Attraction doesn't come on its own. It has to be drawn out. You have to be the worm on the hook, jiggling, for the eyes to bite.

But not everyone drives a classic Vette (or wears a turquoise hat). It can be quite a chore, this quest to Stand Out. But it can be done. Let me put it another way—to generate Surprise, it *MUST* be done. Once you're up from the basement, you have to let people know you've arrived. Don't just tell 'em: shout it out.

Deprogramming time—against the grain we must go (again). All our lives, we've been hard-sold on the virtue of quiet. As babies, we were constantly told to "Hush," to stop crying. As children, we were cautioned that we should be seen, and not heard. Even as adults, the digital world's rules of etiquette frown on EXCESSIVE USE OF CAPITALS lest it disturb all the other poor electronic ones-and-zeroes that are at the root of our e-mails or Tom Peters' books.

In the world of Surprise though, silence is far from golden. In fact, in today's all-pervasive, multimedia business environment, Silence = Death. Even at its most subtle, Surprise is about shouting.

Unfortunately, the act of shouting has endured a bad rap, probably because those who use it most are crass, aggressive boors. Since it's such an integral part of the Surprise lifestyle, that stigma needs to be broken.

Just like paint can be used to create an enduring master-piece or make a revolting mess, when in the right hands, shouting is a deft, expressive tool. (Imagine how ineffective Martin Luther King, Jr. would have been in 1963 had he stood in front of the teeming masses from the steps of the Lincoln Memorial and whispered, "Shhhh . . . I uh, have a dream.")

Shouting doesn't even have to be audible! Used properly, a raised eyebrow can be louder than a jackhammer. It's more about context, and the courage to deviate from the norm, than it is about volume.

Consider the world as made up of periods, commas, and the occasional semicolon; shouting is its very necessary exclamation mark. Like singing, great shouts come from the gut, not the throat. They are inspired, not contrived. Shouting is not necessarily about making you heard. It's about making you interesting—and getting you noticed.

Whenever I am confronted on this conviction of mine (usually by men), I engage my foe in a bloodless duel called "The Wallet Test." The challenge is simple: on the count of three, whip out your wallet and toss it on the table. My wallet these days is a multicolored, thinly-striped billfold from British designer Paul Smith. Its usual opponent, 96 percent of the time at least, is bland, black or brown, absolutely no distinguishing marks, and void of personality. My wallet, on the other hand, sparkles. It's almost electric. It starts conversations. Without saying a word, it shouts out "me" and shouts down the competition. Even more important, internationally-renowned and obsessively-adopted brands like Paul Smith, Chrome Hearts, Modern Amusement, Parasuco and Versace have backboned their businesses on standing out and shouting down others.

The point here is that even with something as inherently mundane as a man's wallet, we're given a choice. And the level of effort that separates Choice A from Choice B is usually marginal, at most. (In the wallet example, all you have to do is point to the striped one instead of the solid one in the display case. Sweating yet?) You can choose to fit in, or choose to Stand Out. You can choose to be boring or exciting. You can choose to walk a shimmering Yellow Brick Road or a dusty dirt path. You can choose to be quiet or to shout.

Cautionary note: shouting isn't 100 percent foolproof. There's always the chance that your next one could backfire. Worse still, if it does, it adheres to the laws of Newtonian physics, where all actions are met with similar or greater reactions. Think of Howard Dean's guttural yelp during the 2004 Presidential race that saw him plummet from hero to zero in the space of a day. (In retrospect though, who would you rather have spent the years 2004 to 2008 in the White House—screamin' Dean, or the relatively reserved Bush?)

The risk is worth it. Actually, the risk is required to move on to the next step to shock and awe. You're about to leave the school of hard knocks. And enter the one of hard shocks. Two things to remember: Think underground. Live over-the-top. Class dismissed.

Summary

CHAPTER 5: THIS WILL BE ON THE EXAM

- Only the loud Surprise; Stand Out or sit down.

- Meetings will be held in the basement. You know who, and you know why.

CHAPTER 6
Let's Hear It for the Surprise Theory Quartet!

At the risk of beatings, prison sentences, and consequences best not discussed in a business book, followers of Chairman Mao not only had to memorize a 33-chapter volume of quotations, but carry it with them at all times. In order to get a handle on one's demons, traditional addiction recovery or behavior modification programs have 12 precise steps to conscientiously abide by. Moving down the numerical scale two notches, Moses trudged down from the mountain with 10 Commandments literally carved in stone for his chosen people to adhere to, which keeps them either in line or guilt-ridden to this very day. In comparison, you have it incredibly easy.

To initiate a flow of eye-popping, talk-inspiring, extreme-expanding Surprise, all you have to keep in mind are the four key theories that permeate just about every action that causes a delight-filled reaction:

1. Everyone's a Kid in Disneyland

2. Balls Beat Brains; Balls Beat Budgets

3. Little Things Mean a Lot

4. Sometimes, There is No Reason

The Surprise Theory Quartet (really does sound like a jazz or retro-pop group, doesn't it?) delves deeper into and expands upon the core values found within all Surprises—the sense of wonderment, the display of guts, the disproportionate reactions, and the constant unpredictability. So divide your brain into quadrants, and get ready to say "Yeah, Yeah, Yeah" to this Fab Four:

1. Everyone's a Kid in Disneyland

This is perhaps the most important of all Surprise theories, hence its position on top of the heap. In essence, theory one declares that Surprise brings out the inner child in *all* of us. Understand and exploit this fact, and half your battle is won.

It works like this: I don't care if you're a CEO of a Fortune 500 company, a resident of a dust-belt trailer park, a tourist from New Guinea, or the frosty cool guitarist for an indie rock band—when you're in Disneyland, you are equal. No matter how important or powerful you are elsewhere, when you're among flying Dumbos and giant Mickey Mice, when you are climbing Space Mountains or dropping from Towers of Terror, you are stripped of all conceit and rank. You may marvel at different things and at different degrees, but you marvel nonetheless. Congregated inside the gilded Disney gates, you have joined the homogeneous mass of wide-eyed, open-mouthed, finger-pointing, popcorn-munching, soda-slurping goofballs.

Not that there's anything wrong with that. Actually, there's a lot *right* with that. That's one of Surprise's primary and most influential functions—it democratizes us by kid-ifying us. By bubbling our inner child up to the surface, Surprise lowers our resistances and weakens our defenses, all while raising our level of happiness. That triple play induces a double-whammy, causing us to act way more emotionally and far less rationally than we would normally. Like Red Bull does to vodka, this mixture of Euphoric Shock and maturity regression ups the potency of Surprise, and in doing so, makes it easier for us to buy things and buy *into* things. And not that there's anything wrong with *that*, either. As film director Billy Wilder once put it: "Everyone in the audience is an idiot, but taken together, they're genius."[1]

The "Happiest Place on Earth," as the Disney parks like to call themselves, are also, on a per-square-foot basis, some of the most cash-flowing places on earth. The correlation is obvious. Attics, closets, and stuff-drawers across the globe are testaments to adorable but relatively unnecessary Disney souvenirs bought in the state of unguarded euphoria. So are waistlines, filled to overflow with high-priced Disney snacks and themed meals. Out of every dollar spent at a Disney park, only 60 percent is spent on admissions; the other 40 percent is spent on merchandise, food, and beverages. Eat, drink, and be merry, indeed!

Away from the parks and closer to home, the "Everyone's a Kid" theory can also be experienced every October 31, when scores of offices, schools, and other edifices where people gather become Disneyland . . . for a day, at least. At my places of work over the past 20 years, every Halloween has been a democratizing occasion where Surprise rules large.

You can hear the squeals of glee as employee after employee comes through the front door in various stages of dress or undress. Some people go against the nature of their personalities, others further exploit their stereotypes, but no matter what unconventional outfit is chosen, the mass enchantment shared as each staffer makes his or her highly anticipated grand appearance is a blast.

Heartwarming yes, but there's something else going on here as well. If your office does dress up days, try this out next Halloween—use that day for "the big ask" you've been somewhat reluctant to attempt otherwise. Other than the week of Christmas, there's no better time to get what you want from your powers that be. The combination of lower resistances, weaker defenses, and elevated happiness may end up paying off big for you ... and allow you to buy a more expensive costume the year after.

The wide-eyed innocence of a child goes way further than most people realize in marketing, and is thus imperative to capture and bottle in the process of generating Surprise. By getting adults to return to their short-pants and lollipop roots, they can find the positive and let the sunshine chase the clouds of cynicism and distrust that may hamper many marketing messages.

The major lesson in theory one is that deep down, grown-ups are at their best, at their most genuine, when being kids. Unfortunately, they just don't get enough chances to be so. When you finally do strip away the titles and offices and social status that tend to classify and differentiate us, you are left with basic human spirits who are essentially impressed and affected by the same things.

To explain, let's take the "Everyone's a Kid in Disneyland" theory out of the parks and into the boardroom. At a Venture

Capital conference a couple years ago, I was fascinated by a speech made by Dr. Richard Bruno, a university professor turned venture capitalist (VC). Of particular interest in Dr. Bruno's dissertation was his "Business Plans to Bucks" timeline, in which he took entrepreneurs down this startling path of reality:

- 🍄 1,000 Business Plans Are Written

- 🍄 150 Are Moderately Credible

- 🍄 50 Are Interesting To Read

- 🍄 20 Undergo Due Diligence

- 🍄 5 Get Funded

- 🍄 1 Makes Money

The big shock here is not that only one business in every 1,000 actually turns a profit; the big shock is that "Interesting to Read" is a fundamental VC criteria.

Many times, as entrepreneurs try to appeal to their corporate audience, their brilliant ideas are sanded down and neutered by VC-speak. Notwithstanding their typecast reputations, Venture Capitalists are not robots; they are (for the most part) human beings like you and I, and are as susceptible to the right excitement, creativity, and sell job as the next guy. At Disneyland, they will also point at Dumbo. Given the proper party invite, they will also dress up on Halloween. And like you or I, given a choice, they would rather read something interesting than something stultifying.

Theory one is also why the Madonna Inn is still around, almost a half-century after its audacious inception; the place is akin to living in a storybook, albeit at a couple of hundred bucks a night. No relation to the singer, the San Luis Obispo, California hotel is comprised of 109 very different rooms, each with its own décor and story. Despite the tremendous competition in the area (it's literally halfway between San Francisco and Los Angeles in the state's lush central coast region), travelers go out of their way to spend a night or two in land-of-make-believe accommodations that are made of rocks, feature moonshine stills or stagecoach beds, or are painted in hues so shocking that you'll need solar eclipse-grade sunglasses when you open the door. It's the antithesis of the hipster boutique hotels, and it ain't cheap either. People pay nicely for the experience, take scads of pictures and videos, buy the perfunctory souvenirs, and blog incessantly about their stays. When was the last time you saw someone blog about a Marriott or a Hilton or a Ramada ... other than to complain about it?

Not every hotel can redo each room, but even by redoing just one, they can benefit from the buzz by giving people something to point at. Speaking at a Hotel Management conference last year, I recommended to the assembled operators that they outfit at least one of their rooms with the furniture creations of someone like Judson Beaumont, who owns a company called Straight Line Designs. Judson creates the type of tables, armoires, and cabinets that one can only dream of ... after reading a Dr. Seuss book, traipsing through a Salvador Dali retrospective, watching an episode of Pee Wee Herman, and eating some very special mushrooms. These pieces don't just store clothing or provide a surface to lay down an hors d'oeuvre; they inspire oohs, ahhs, pictures, and stories. See Figures 6.1 through 6.3 for a look.

Figure 6.1 Bad Table 2005, 40″ W ×
18″ H × 20″ D, Stained Maple &
Veneer Aluminum Pee, Ikea Carpet,
(Photo by Ken Mayer)

Figure 6.2 Oops! 2008, 29″ W × 38″ H
× 16″ D, Maple & Veneer, (Photo by Mike
Wakefield)

Figure 6.3 Boom Cabinet 2007, 21″ W × 52″ H × 12″ D, Stained Maple & Veneer, (Photo by Mike Wakefield)

Crazy, huh? Now let's say that someone in the conference crowd actually took my advice and steadfastly applied it. I *guarantee* that this one hotel room of theirs will be the one requested by travelers, the one with a waiting list, and the one that will become the hotel's calling card. Frankly, the hotel wouldn't even have to let someone sleep in this room; just letting people come in and take pictures in it would be more than enough. Making adults feel like kids goes a long way in the hospitality biz. The Doubletree Hotel chain is renowned worldwide, not for anything having to do with its level of comfort or service, but by its simple childhood-regressive act of giving away warm chocolate chip cookies at check-in (milk not included . . . but should be).

Everyone is indeed a kid when in Disneyland. And by creating Surprise, you're providing the (it's a small) world with a front-of-the line, VIP season's pass.

2. Balls Beat Brains, Balls Beat Budgets

I often think back to what brought me to my first marketing course back in college. I was there purely by happenstance; the Psych class I really wanted to take was full, and Marketing 101 (seriously, it really was called that!) just so happened to fit the one open time slot in my schedule. The move was both serendipitous and lucky, as not only did this course set me on my life's path and passion, but it introduced me to the best teacher I've ever known, a sage retired food executive named Don Tobin, who was giving back to the community by teaching entry-level marketing to long-haired greenhorns like me. One central factor that Don stressed throughout the course was the nature of controlled versus uncontrolled variables, and how the latter will always overpower the former.

Don has sadly long passed on, but looking down from that great corner office in the sky he is smiling broadly, because in today's game of business, the ultimate trump card has been played: these days, it's *ALL* uncontrollable variables. The oft-heard refrain among the cognoscenti of business 2.0 is, "There is no control!" Indeed, even thinking that one could have power over a variable shows either the love of a paradox or a most lofty sense of conceit.

Given this, we come to theory two in Surprise marketing. In a world where everything has spun out of control, you can plan obsessively, cross every "t," dot every "i," and still be obliterated by something even the most subversive science-fiction writer, in his wildest imagination, could never conceive. Marketing in a world like ours poses problems and exposes opportunities that can't be dealt with simply by throwing more money at them or spending more time thinking through them. Marketing in a world like ours requires a psyche that takes advantage of the personality traits we discussed in Chapter 5.

This is why I say that Big Balls Beat both Brains and Budgets. (And I say it five times fast.) Smart people, while incredibly valuable, won't necessarily change the world. Yes, they will ultimately rule it and run it, but they will do so for the guy or girl with enough guts to do the something they never would in a cajillion years. As for those who drip cash, I send this sage warning that was uttered *sotto voce* to me by an early investor in Airborne Mobile: "They who the Gods want to destroy are given unlimited budgets."

It seems to be standard operating procedure in business that inevitably, a successful company grows beyond the authority of the entrepreneur who started it, and the panicked Bat-signaled call goes out for "Professional Management!" to save the day. Not that this is all that bad, but without the (now) out-of-their-league visionary, there would be no business to professionally manage in the first place. The smart folks need the ballsy ones as a jumpstart.

Note that there is really no such thing as a "Professional Entrepreneur" (although the call for a wild-eyed game-changer by stifled, stuck-in-their-ways companies is something this book officially endorses). Unlike management, entrepreneurship is not necessarily a skill that can be learned; it is a calling that must be heeded. Like somewhat mad, take-no-prisoner outlaws, true entrepreneurs are described as serial, not professional.

I recently spent a day at one of those Future of Mobile Media seminars, and plunked myself down front row at a midday panel session featuring a trio of the field's most powerful executives (I'd name names, but since my company is still working with their companies, there's a limit to my suicidal tendencies). Listening to these three whip-smart captains of the corporate world, I was impressed with their knowledge of the space, but depressed by their lack of vision, new ideas, or "follow me!" leadership. They were great at describing what ails the industry, at making excuses for what wasn't working, but after an interminable 90 minutes, they offered no solutions, or real hope, for the future.

Contrast that to a couple of relatively unkempt, bright-eyed individuals (the literal embodiment of the "two kids in a garage" cliché) who, a little earlier in the day, laid out their dicey, but stimulating, blueprints for tomorrow in an uneven yet fascinating half hour. Once they were done, you had to beg people to come back into the ballroom for the next panel because the line to talk to them individually and sign up for their dreams had begun spontaneously and instantaneously as they left the podium.

Think about this the next time someone inspires you. Is it the smartest person in the room? Or the most courageous? Einstein said that "Imagination is more important than knowledge." And as smart as *he* was, he had even bigger balls.

Smart people follow the rules, the directions; ballsy people follow their hearts. Every time I repeat that adage, I remember a call I got from my elder son Aidan when he was 20.

He was attending a marketing conference on a student pass to hear Seth Godin speak, and had stumbled upon an opportunity upon leaving Seth's session.

"Dad," he whispered, "I'm walking around the display and demo area, and I see that there's an empty table here. Do you think I'd get in trouble if I filled it with my business cards?"

While I appreciated his concern about pissing off the organizers who were kind enough to get him a discounted rate, my advice was simple: "Get in trouble for what? Marketing yourself at a marketing conference? Go to it, but don't just throw them there. Do something that says 'you.'" End result— the artistic display of Aidan's business cards (he's into music marketing, so he laid out his cards to look like a giant half-note) peeved the folks at the next table who paid $2,000 for the same privilege, but earned him a job interview and the first client for his social networking consulting business.

During my tenure at the very tightly-budgeted Just For Laughs, my colleague Bruce Hills and I, armed only with Festival swag and a smile, used to regularly cajole First-Class overseas flight upgrades. "Any schmuck can spend $12,000 for a First-Class ticket to London," we used to say, "but it takes balls to sit right next to him for a $319 economy fare, a stuffed puppet, and a couple of Just For Laughs t-shirts." Same thing goes in modern marketing. Anyone with deep pockets can spend zillions on a major media campaign, but it takes someone special to do something Surprising on a shoestring that people will talk about.

Regrettably, ever since the 2007 Adult Swim bomb scare/flashing sign debacle in Boston, the concept of "guerrilla marketing" has been tarred with the bad rap brush, but do the math—it's the ball-swinging marketers that bend, break, or rewrite the rules who reap the most rewards (and don't forget that the root word of "guerrilla" is "guerre," which is French for "war," so . . .).

I remember in the early days of Airborne Mobile, when we could hardly afford to attend conferences—let alone have a booth or a table or be an official "sponsor" of them—we used to pull all sorts of under-the-radar, big-ball stunts to grab attention and promote our cell phone entertainment. One of the most effective, and most fun, involved a pair of cheap wire cutters we attached to a card and called Airborne's "ConVertix 3.3 Wireless Conversion Kit." That's it in all its glory in Figure 6.4. The card read:

> *Converts entertainment to wireless in a snap!*
> *Perfect for cutting your ties to old media models.*
> *Helpful for convincing others to convert, especially when applied to fleshy areas.*

Our secret agent-esque M.O. would see us jam as many wire cutters as we could into a soft briefcase, sneak into keynote rooms or demo/display areas, and place them on every seat or empty spot we could find. Did it work? Well, after doing the dirty deed myself at a conference at the Beverly Hilton in Los Angeles back in 2000 (pre-9/11, which meant I could travel quite freely with a bag filled with wire cutters), I was stopped by two people in the halls.

"Are you the guy behind all those pliers?" bitched one. She was one of the event's organizers. "If I catch you doing that again, I will have you thrown out of here!" she threatened with a screech.

Figure 6.4 A nuisance to some, a calling card to others.

Gulp. Skulking away sheepishly, looking to take refuge in the Hilton's bathroom, I was approached a second time as I fled down the corridors. "Are you the guy behind all those pliers?" I was asked again. But this time, it was an executive from Disney named Tripp Wood. "I think they're great," he beamed. "I love 'em. In fact, I'd like to set up a meeting with you and see how we can work together." I was at his office the next day and the glorious end result here was a contract to create a mobile game for the film *Monsters, Inc.* That meeting with Tripp spawned a friendship that lasts until this day, as well as a five-year professional relationship with Disney that brought us our first big client, immediately established Airborne's credibility, and gave us the heat needed to sign up clients like HBO, Maxim, A&E, the NHL, and The Food Network within a year.

Despite the image of swinging wildly from the trees and the homonym with "guerilla," the Surprise marketer's true mascot is the antithesis of the 800-pound ape. In fact, as I slithered my way through the Hilton hallways that fateful day, I realized that a big-balled entrepreneur is less of a jungle beast and more of an aquatic eel.

Just think about it. Here's a slippery fish that looks like a giant worm, but acts like a vicious snake. Despite their relatively modest outward appearance, eels are mean mofos; almost all of them are predators of the first degree, and if hungry enough, will even eat their own siblings and offspring (which must make eel family reunions a harrowing experience). The electric eel varieties of the species are capable of generating powerful shocks, which they use for hunting and self-defense. And although they lack pelvic fins and the associated skeletal structures common to their fish family, eels manage to rip through the water at speeds up to 20 miles per hour.

No ivory towers for these guys, either. The CEO-like sharks may get their own week of glory on the Discovery Channel, but it's the eels who are the unsung streetfighters of marketing. So let's compare the qualities common to both the entrepreneur and the eel:

- Deceptively dangerous

- Fast as hell

- Hungry like the wolf

- Tough as nails

- Hard to catch (despite the sushi . . .)

The most important factor though, and greatest similarity between eel and entrepreneur, is *HOW* they move. Yes, the eel is a speedy little critter. It knows where it wants to go, and gets there fast. But never in a straight line.

The wiggle of the eel is an important part of its physiology and its survival—same with an entrepreneur. Having your eyes on the prize, but not being glued to a set roadmap and direction, is what separates the successes from the failures. True entrepreneurs roll with the punches . . . and there are many of them. Markets swing, tastes change, and general shift just happens. True entrepreneurs can change direction often and rapidly, without losing sight of where they're going. And know how to get back there if they're knocked wildly off course. And know how to find a new place to go if the original destination is blocked (just like the eels do it).

They are the species best equipped to deal with today's whirlpool of uncontrollable variables. Who needs the comfort of control when you've the balls to embrace chaos?

3. Little Things Mean A Lot

The key paradox about Surprise is one of the most important elements in creating it. As theory two established, yes, your balls have to be big. But what you do with them doesn't have to be. That's the essential root of theory three—the disproportionate power of the "little thing." (Big balls, little things . . . there's something strangely Freudian going on here.)

When I first discussed this incongruous theory with colleagues, the standard immediate reaction was, "Oh, you mean that 'less is more.'" No, not really. Less is, without a doubt, less. In generating Surprise, it's best to heed the advice of design deity Milton Glaser (visual maestro behind the "I♥NY" image, among other cultural iconography), who once said, "Less isn't more, just enough is more."[2]

I couldn't agree, uh, more. Glaser is an esteemed role model in creating Surprise, for what is Surprise if not the design of an unforgettable experience? Overdo it and you turn people off; underdo it and you leave them nonplussed and yawning. "Just enough" isn't a compromise when it comes to designing Surprise. It's the optimum sweet spot that delivers the unexpected but leaves 'em wanting (aww, here we go again!) more.

Theory three raises skeptical hackles when talked about, but manages to impress when acted upon. A great example is how blogger Ryan Karpeles niftily recants a Pow! Moment he experienced in a restaurant. While the payoff was minimal, the impact of something as minute as utensil placement begat this inspired post:

> *You walk into a fancy restaurant. You're ushered to your table and the host pulls out a seat for you. As you sit down and scoot your chair forward, you notice something rather peculiar . . .* ***The forks are on the right side of your plate, and the knife and spoon are on the left.***

Your brain skips a beat. Your thoughts freeze in time. Everything you thought you knew about proper utensil placement has been turned upside down. Was this a mistake? Do they always do this?

Then you look at everyone else's silverware. It's all backwards too. What in the world is going on? How dare these people buck the place-setting system? But guess what. They made you notice. They got your attention. You'll probably even tell several people about the dyslexic silverware incident as soon as you get a chance. And the best part? It cost absolutely nothing.

Of course it will help if the food is great. But dining out is only partially about the meal. The service, the atmosphere, the aesthetics and loads of other factors play a pivotal role in your overall experience.

Believe it or not, something as simple as flipping the eating utensil arrangement can have a lasting impact. **This is the paradox. People notice tiny changes before they recognize massive shifts. Trees first. Forest second.**[3]

Isn't that grand? "Trees first. Forest second." In a mere four words, the coda to Ryan's ode to silverware set-up sums up the soul of theory three. One may dismiss Ryan's philosophical waxing as some sort of freaky fork fetish, but I have also experienced the type of reaction a skewed cutlery conundrum can cause. I had just finished a speaking engagement headlined by Anthony Robbins in Vancouver, and I took the family up to Whistler, B.C. for a few days of snowboarding.

The first night, during dinner at Milestone's restaurant, I noticed the people at the table facing ours pointing in my general direction. At first, I thought they might have recognized me from the speech, but when I saw another tableful of people point as well, I figured the odds of all these people being at the same speech to be infinitesimal, so with deflated ego, I turned around to see at what else they could be pointing. What I discovered can be seen in Figures 6.5 and 6.6.

Figure 6.5

Directly behind me were three colorful, framed lithographs of cutlery, but audaciously mislabeled (i.e., the knife as a spoon, the fork as a knife).While the images themselves were kind of cool and quite tasteful, they were as innocuous as the thousands of other images that adorn

Figure 6.6

restaurant walls ad infinitum. But that little touch of incongruity made them into conversation pieces, and something to point at as well. In the grand scheme of things, this is silly, inconsequential. But the notion to ponder is this: When was the last time *YOU* pointed at anything on a restaurant wall?

Chapter 2 gave you the examples of the bookstore-line chocolates and the hotel workout wear cleaning service. Here are a few others that will explain this theory way more effectively than any further hypothesizing and philosophizing:

While in Vancouver for the aforementioned Tony Robbins gig, I was put up at the Pan Pacific Hotel. Fine place, wonderful service . . . exactly what you'd expect for $500 a night. What was unexpected was the way the floors in the elevators changed every day (well, at least the inlaid floor mats did). If

Figure 6.7   Look down and strike up a conversation.

you're hungover, or suffering from multi-time-zone jet lag, all you have to do to get your bearings straight is take a quick peek down (See Figure 6.7).

Given my travel history, I've been in thousands of hotel elevators over the years and have never seen anything else—ads, glass walls, music, you name it!—that spawned smiles and actual *conversation* between riders. The usual focal point of elevators is up at the changing floor numbers; here, it's down on the changing floor letters.

Being known as the Prince of Pow! does have its benefits. Ryan Karpeles's tale is just the tip of the iceberg; people from all over the world (I call them "Friends of Pow!" or FOPs) have converted my blog and email inbox into repositories for examples of the Surprise marketing that moves them, most notably the little things that go unnoticed by the mainstream business press.

One of my favorites was sent by military technologist Dan Ward, who sent me the story of being blown away by something as commonplace as a box of Bounce Fabric Softener. "My wife opened a new box, and inside was a small white envelope," Dan wrote. Inside the envelope was a card that said the following:

Dear Friend
At Bounce, we believe even the little things should brighten your day. So on our 35th US and 31st Canadian anniversaries, we'd simply like to thank you for choosing Bounce.
Thank you!
Everyone at Bounce

Dan went on to say that his wife "thought it was cool enough to mention it to me. And many others. I figure that's got to count for something."

Wrongo. It doesn't count for something; it counts for everything. When was the last time anyone made a fuss over fabric softener? And this isn't even about fabric softener; it's about a massive conglomerate putting on a human face by sending its faithful clients a little, unexpected note. This initiative cost Procter & Gamble a fraction more than nothing, and just the fact that it's mentioned here already makes the company's investment a wise one. That it elicited tens of thousands more smiles and verbal or written exchanges makes it a brilliant one.

As I noted at the outset of this book, for the past four years, I've spent my Christmas vacations snowboarding in Vail. For those who have never been, it's a snow-lover's heaven, a mammoth mountain cuffed by a town filled with the finest of restaurants (national cuisine award-winners like Kelly Liken and Sweet Basil to name just two), trend-setting boutiques (like Due and Luca Bruno) and some of the coolest, quirkiest places to see and be seen.

But every time I mention to fellow Vail visitors that I'm staying in a complex called Lionshead Arcade, they seem to ask: "Isn't that where the French Deli is?"

Now this French Deli is far from unique. It serves sandwiches, cappuccino, bags of chips, and other foodstuff staples. So do dozens of other places here. What makes it stand out is its rather eccentric opening hours, as seen in Figure 6.8.

Figure 6.8   No such thing as "fashionably-late" here.

The weirdness of 7:44 a.m. and 4:01 p.m., as ridiculous as it may sound, means way more than anything The French Deli serves. I've overheard people talking about it all over town— in lift lines, in stores, even at the local Starbucks. (And these guys stick to their guns, too. My son once went down for a coffee at about 4:10. Zut alors! Closed tight.)

The Eagles sang, "In a New York minute, everything can change." Well, in a Vail minute, everyone takes notice.

Since we're on the subject of snowboarding, hard-core riders may swear by more independent brands, but nobody sells more boards or gear than Burton, Jake Burton Carpenter's Vermont-based, industry pioneer. Reason why? The company's design, branding, and use of color never fail to

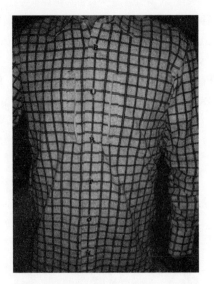

Figure 6.9   The branding is in
the buttons.

open eyes. Even when they are toned down, they never fail
to be audacious. Case in point is this Burton shirt shown in
Figure 6.9—nice . . . but somewhat traditional and standard.
Until you take a closer look at the buttons, that is.

And most people certainly do lean in for that closer look.
They smile, and ask about it ("Did it come like that or did
you do it?", "Are they still available?", "How much was it?").
Between my two sons and me, we must have about 20 pieces
of Burton apparel. Other than this one, where the branding
is so subtle it needs to be pointed out, not one of them ever
produced as much as a word of feedback.

Louis Tetu is a very bright man. He conceives, builds, and
sells companies (like Taleo, the NASDAQ-listed talent management software firm), and then looks for the next challenge.

Louis Tetu
Executive Chairman
Father. Skier. Pilot. Wine enthusiast.

((C O V E O ™

2800 St. Jean-Baptiste Ave., Suite 212
Québec (QC) G2E 6J5 Canada

T. +1-418-263-1111
F. +1-418-263-1221
ltetu@coveo.com
www.coveo.com

Figure 6.10 Four points, five words, hundreds of ways to relate.

And he understands the power of little things intrinsically. At a recent tech entrepreneur dinner, Louis caused quite a stir by passing out his business card, seen in Figure 6.10. The five extra words below his official title spawned waves of chatter; some about Louis (most, however, was good-natured envy about the card itself).

Without any splash of color or die-cut gimmickry (not that there's anything wrong with that, however), Louis's card was the talk of the night. Of his understated five word "subtitle," he explained that it serves not only as statement to who he is as an individual (i.e., *not* just a businessman), but manages to act as a "connector" to those he meets, establishing points in common to build relationships, not just business. What's more, he insists that every last one of his 700-or-so employees do the same and list four personal attributes on their cards.

It's neither fancy, nor earth-shattering ... but by now, you know it doesn't have to be. You don't expect to see anything "personal" on "business" cards, never mind four or five words that provide an insight to one's psyche. Thanks to Google, anyone who just wants to find your address or phone number can do so instantly. Rather than just be entered into a database or tacked on to a Rolodex (ask your parents), Louis proves that business cards today can have a greater purpose.

Displaced or misnamed cutlery. Calendar carpets. Small, secret notes. Sixty seconds. Six letters. Five words.

With all due respect to author Dr. Richard Carlson, it seems that much can be gained from sweating the small stuff. Go ahead and keep sweating 'em.

4. Sometimes, There Is No Reason

"Why."

It is the word chosen to jumpstart the most popular questions in business.

"Why would we do this?"

"Why did we try that?"

"Why can't we go there?"

"Why should we choose them?"

Many times, the question is simply the word itself; no other accompaniment necessary.

"Why?"

It's instinctive in the corporate arena to pose questions ... and equally as instinctive to expect answers. Asking "Why?" is a staple of demonstrating one's search for common knowledge, a piece of standard operating procedure, recognized as part of a company's best practices.

Sometimes, not often enough though, there is no "Why?" Sometimes, the only reason one needs is "Because."

The beauty of "Because" is that it doesn't always need to be followed with a proper explanation. Given enough support, "Because" is often strong enough to stand on its own—especially when you want to generate Surprise.

The rules are different here. Forget the teachings of MIT Sloan School of Management's Doug McGregor; his human motivation hypotheses Theory X and Theory Y have been replaced by Theory "Why Not?" that believes that all people are fundamentally crazy. In the Tao of Pow!, you need to embrace "Because" while eschewing explanation and reason. Rational justification will lead you to the (com)promised land of the standard, the humdrum, the same. That's not our preferred destination.

In generating Surprise, "Because" is the new "Why?" Why do I say this? Because.

Because of people like Sami Bay, the 31-year-old founder of SomethingStore.com. Something in the way he moves goods attracts me like no other retailer. Many smart sellers (particularly those who have purchased this book) exploit the element of Surprise to drive business, but at Sami's SomethingStore, Surprise *IS* its business. The concept is as simple as can be:

1. You send them $10.

2. They send you something in return (shipping and handling is included in the $10).

The store's inventory is a random selection of stuff; "Somethings" can include anything from a magnetic dart board to a Bluetooth headset to a $25 BestBuy gift card to a shrink-wrapped copy of Madden '08. And this is not a recycling of somebody else's secondhand junk. Bay acquires his goods from wholesalers he met while working at another Internet retailer, from a network of liquidators and, on an increasingly frequent basis, from manufacturers looking to seed their products via sampling. The company doesn't specify what it will send, but given the extensive detail of what it will NOT (its "Something Not" list of verboten products includes adult entertainment, body parts, counterfeit goods, weapons, and miracle cures), the end result seems to be something relatively upbeat and harmless, providing a substantial bang for ten bucks. The margins are nothing to sneeze at either, generally running at about 30 percent, and on the rise due to the uptick in sampling popularity.

"I got the idea when I was jumping around websites searching for a gift," says Bay of his brainchild's origin. "After over an hour of looking for that perfect 'something,' I realized that it would be easier—and more fun—to send some sort of random product where even I wouldn't know what it was."[4]

Launched in November 2007, SomethingStore.com chugged along gradually until the tipping point of Mother's Day 2008. The undeniably off-beat concept gave the mass media a new angle for its annual Groundhog Day-like story about the maternal holiday, and suddenly . . . well, by now, you should know the drill: word of mouth, bloggers, attention, rapidly rising revenue.

Throughout the climb, Bay stayed true to his roots; he understands what his customers are really buying.

"I'm selling Surprise," he says. "Pure and simple."

There is no reason. There is no rhyme. The answer to the puzzled "Why?" is the flippant "Because." And the "Because" seems to be resonating deeply. If Costco's Chapter 4 description was "a retail treasure hunt," SomethingStore.com's is akin to a house of worship; a funhouse of worship, more likely. Some of Bay's customer reviews and testimonials read like a nitrous oxide-infused revival meeting:

> *"Wonderful idea in so many ways, you may not even be aware of!"*
> *"Awesome business plan, and really fun to just see what shows up."*
> *"We wanted a surprise and that is what we got!"*

Bay's favorite and most poignant tale of customer satisfaction comes from a woman in New Jersey, who was loyal in her consistent ordering of a new "Something" every two weeks. Noticing the pattern and devotion, Bay sent the woman a personal thank you note. The response touched him deeply.

"She was chronically ill and alone," Bay explains, "and looked forward to getting a surprise in the mail to brighten up her day every two weeks."

In the process, it did the same for Bay. "I believe in the potential and the scalability of this business," he says, "but what's really something is being able to make a difference in somebody's life."[5]

Now, for no other reason than "Because I can," let me introduce you to the King of Literary Segues, who is here with this transition:

And speaking of "making a difference
in somebody's life . . ."

. . . I bring you the story of Suzanne Hinks, yet another one of those personal examples that fill my file cabinets, thumb drives, and ultimately, this book. Suzanne was a very young lady from Calgary who reached out to me in 1998 when I was CEO of Just For Laughs. In her typewritten letter, written on a whim after seeing our fifteenth anniversary TV special, she expressed her love for and knowledge of the comedic arts, and said she would pull up roots and move to Montreal for a job at the festival.

It just so happened that at the time, I was looking for a new assistant to help me through the summer, so without ever meeting her face-to-face, without any due diligence of any sort, I just called her up and said "Yes;" pure blind faith. Why? Once again, because I could. The reactions were varied, but swift.

Suzanne couldn't believe her ears when I gave her the go-ahead. She was ebullient and stunned at the same time. When *she* asked why, I told her that she sounded sincere in her letter, that I had nothing to lose (hey, *she* was the one moving across the country on a whim, not me), and most importantly, that I wanted her to believe in taking the shot and prove that sometimes, even the most implausible dreams do come true. Even had the Just For Laughs job not worked out in the end, for the rest of her life, Suzanne would be able to tell the story of how she wrote this letter, and how she never thought she would even get a response, never mind a personal phone call with an immediate job offer. Best of all, maybe one day she would be in the position to do the same for some other young, doe-eyed hopeful.

At the office however, the response was, shall we say, a little less enthusiastic. I was called "insane," "irresponsible," "an idiot" . . . and those were just the words starting with "I" (good thing I was CEO, or else things could've gotten *really* nasty). I was told that this broke all the procedural rules set up by our HR department on the proper manner in which to engage staff, and in doing so, made a mockery of those currently in the employ of the company. "If you can just hire anyone off the street," I was chided, "what does that say about the value of those who are already working here?" (My response of "At one time, we were all 'just anyone off the street'" did not go far in smoothing ruffled feathers.)

Well, in the grandest Surprise tradition, the system was most definitely shocked. Good thing, because things in good humor-land were getting a little stale and complacent, and were in desperate need of a positive shake-up. Suzanne came in from Cow-town (as we easterners derisively called Calgary) with her one suitcase of inappropriately conservative clothing, knowing nobody, with nowhere to live . . . and quickly carved out her spot. Those who resented and doubted her soon fell victim to her innocent, unassuming manner and get-things-done-with-a-chuckle attitude. Today, more than a decade later, "Hinksie" is still at Just For Laughs, promoted upstairs to the position of the company's Operations Manager, where she has her finger on the pulse of everything except booking the acts. As an epilogue, ask her how she herself hired a young New Yorker named Henry Kaiser. But don't ask her "Why?"

One of TV's most popular shows, the very rich Seth McFarlane's animated hit *Family Guy*, owes part of its success to the shunning of "Why" and compulsive exploitation of "Because." Episodes are rife with *non sequiturs* (the Latin for "it does not follow") that interrupt the story's flow (which is relatively disjointed in the first place) and flash over to totally unrelated anecdotes and scenes. A recurring fan favorite is an increasingly lengthy and progressively more violent fistfight between household head Peter Griffin and a giant chicken . . . which makes total sense to anyone who has ever seen the show.

Although I shy away from oversized poultry, I try to play the "Because" card all the time in my day-to-day life. Not on a regular basis, never scheduled, but I harness its off-centering power whenever the whim hits me. I recently called an old friend who I haven't spoken to in well over a year. His name is Frank Supovitz, and he's the Senior VP of Events for the National Football League, a job that's been called "one of the biggest anywhere in event management." Frank gets thousands of calls and emails a week, and if they're not about fires to put out, they're about requests for tickets or passes to something big that he's doing. This is the message I left on his voicemail:

> *Frank, it's Andy Nulman. Guess what? I don't need anything. I'm not calling for tickets to the Super Bowl, for passes to the season opening party, for a donation to a silent auction, nothing! I'm just calling to say hi because we haven't spoken in a while. Hope all is well. Call me back if you can.*

I got a return call before the afternoon was up. "Because" trumps all reasoning, ignites the Euphoric Shock of Surprise, and more often than not, is a welcome breath of fresh air in the daily windstorm of halitosis.

Don't believe me yet? Then try it yourself—right now. Call or email someone you haven't called or emailed in a while, and measure their delight when you tell them that there's no reason for touching base; you were "just thinking about them."

Or if you're ready to haul out the big guns, take this one step further, and bring theory four to your place of work. Here's what to do: choose someone you do business with. It could be one of your best clients/customers, or someone at random from your opt-in or email list (finally, a chance to use it!), but focus in on just one. Next step is to call or email this lucky person with the following offer:

Come into my (store, catalog, site, salon, etc.) and choose any one item/service you want for free. No conditions. No questions asked.

Then watch the fun begin. This simple call or email is a highly personal outreach, one of those little things that will, without a doubt, mean a lot to your person of choice (theory three, if you recall). When they rub their eyes, pull out a microscope to check the fine print, pinch themselves, call their lawyers to see if there's some sort of catch, and ultimately, incredulously ask "Why?", just say: "Because I value your business and wanted to do something nice for one of my customers."

This should not be a coordinated effort with your other marketing plans. This should not be prepromoed or advertised as "Coming Soon!" It should be coming all right, but from out of the blue. Totally unexpected. Just because.

The offer you're making is a ballsy one; don't be afraid to pump up your orbs to the size of weather balloons with it (theory two, for those keeping score). You're not tossing someone a flimsy promotional t-shirt or chintzy logoed pen, you are giving free reign to your shelves, your warehouse, your professional services. Give up control and let big things happen.

No matter what item or service your customer will eventually choose, no matter where it is positioned on the price spectrum, the rewards you will receive will be disproportionately weighted in your favor. Even if you're a car dealer and you're on the hook for a shiny new vehicle, the WOM and PR that this one tiny-but-powerful offer will exponentially surpass your cost in it (which gives rise to a new term: "The Womper," the blending of Word of Mouth buzz and Public Relations coverage that results in acute attention and a stately return on investment).

You don't need to make a big deal about this; your customer will make a big deal about it for you. You don't need to alert the media; your customer will generate so much noise that they'll be tracking you down instead. Just make the call or send the email. Then sit back and enjoy that slightly bewildered look, that tentative excitement, that visible heart flutter when your customer finally enters your place of business to concretize your most incredible and generous offer.

They'll look just like a kid—in Disneyland.

Summary

The Fab Four of Chapter 6

- Fortune 500 CEO or trailer park doyen, fashion model or punk rocker, it doesn't matter—we're all the same in Disneyland.

- Oversize your risk-taking—pound your chest like a gorilla and slither like an eel.

- Remember the law of disproportion in Surprise—little things mean a lot.

- Suppress the need to ask "Why?" Instead, embrace the freedom of doing things "Because."

CHAPTER 7
The Art of the Business of Creating Surprise

At this juncture in the book, I feel like one of those overweight roadie-cum-announcers at a heavy metal concert. Since we have established what Surprise is and what it ain't, marveled at its power, confronted its conundrum, delved into the headspace, and studied the theories needed to create it, all that's really left to do is fill my lungs with oxygen, slick back my shoulder-length hair, saunter up to the mic stand, grab it with all the finesse of a madman strangling a stork, and bellow with tornado-force breath:

"Alright readers!
Wherever you are!
Are you ready to rock?"

It's time to do it.

The next phase in your education process is the fundamental "How-To" training. But there's a slight hiccup before we proceed. Despite the fact that this tome may have been classified as a "Business" book by the literary powers that be, frankly, the actual act of creating Surprise is more at home in the world of art than in the world of business.

That said, there are two schools of thought when it comes to the teaching of art. Think of the debate as a Mark Rothko painting. On one side of the very expensive colored line are the traditionalists who believe that art is a process, and thus can be taught in educational institutions. On the other side are the freethinkers like Marshall McLuhan and Andy Warhol (let's call them the "An-art-chists"), both who have been credited with uttering the phrase "Art is anything you can get away with."

Given our ultimate goal of expanding the boundaries of delightful extremes, the freethinkers seem to be more in synch with the spirit of Pow! than their more rigid brethren (and more in synch with yours truly as well). I've always said that you don't "study" marketing as much as you actually live it. Over the past 25 years, an oft-heard battle cry around my offices has been: "Get off the floor and out the door!" In other words, go outside and watch how people are shopping, what they're buying, what they're wearing, eating, drinking, listening to, and so forth. Pretend you're a visitor from another planet trying to get a read on this strange race called the American Consumer. Your personal observations and reactions are equally as, if not more, valuable than anything you can ever learn in a marketing classroom.

Learning how to Surprise is like learning how to kiss, or how to fall in love; eventually, you just have to take the plunge, and know that as time marches on, you'll get better with practice. Unlike doing the Hokey-Pokey, there is no "right foot in/left foot out" step-by-step procedure. Still spinning with the dance analogy, Surprise is more like Krumping or Popping (ask your kids), where you are given the liberty to try whatever you want. You can take what has already been done and add your own personal style to it, or you can do what's never even been attempted before. Go crazy; both the Surprise and the Krumping police forces have long been retired.

So if we have to redefine the mission of this chapter, it's not necessarily a "How-To" as much as it is a "How They"—a deep and diverse collection of tactics and ideas from others that will inspire you to launch your own.

Before we move on with this bountiful cornucopia of tactics and ideas, an important aside: by tossing laurels at the freethinkers and fast-doers, I'm not dissing those who have methodically broken down the process of idea generation. In fact, two of the best that I use on a regular basis to unstick my own mind come from Doug Hall and Roger von Oech. Over a quarter-century ago, Roger wrote what I consider to be the ultimate creativity classic with *A Whack on the Side of the Head,* a selection of mental jump-starters that open up doors of perception you never before noticed were there (his follow-up volume, *A Kick in the Seat of the Pants,* is equally filled with ways and means to see and act differently). Doug's process is a little more involved (requiring random words, Post-It notes, 20-sided dice, and three-way linking of new ideas), but he uses them to stimulate new concepts from the outside-in, which is way more effective—and fun—than the usual regurgitation of stale ideas already stuck in our head known as "Brainstorming." The point, though, is that these admirable books have already been written, and Roger's and Doug's works are great teammates to this one.

The most important tips that I can give you to spark your own Surprise machines are short in scope but deep in practice:

1. To create Surprise, start by following the traditional road. Then look for the fork.

2. Consider life to be the round hole. Your job is to be the square peg.

3. If you're still too conservative or traditional to look for forks or to be a peg, then find someone who is not.

4. This sounds wacky, but it's the most important of the bunch: believe in a greater creative force. Most ideas come on their own when you least expect them. Stop looking so hard. Have faith that they will find you. They will. In her book *Uncommon Genius,* Denise Shek-erjian examines how ideas are born with 40 winners of the MacArthur Foundation Fellowship (a.k.a., "The Genius Award"). One of their key points is simply, stay loose. "Creative people," she says, "are more willing to entertain a prolonged period of leisurely drifting about, curious to see where the unpredictable currents will take them. From this lightness of spirit come the fruits of imagination."[1]

Aw jeez, will you look at that! I've just come up with a step-by-step procedure to construct Surprise. And that's what I suspect you'll find in your search for ideas—they'll congregate around and eventually engulf you before you know what hit you. Like the flywheel so neatly described by Jim Collins in *Good to Great,* coming up with ideas will be arduous the first few go-rounds, but after the initial two or three spins of the heavy wheel, perpetual motion takes over and the ideas will multiply like the proverbial rabbits. Finding ideas will soon become easy. The tough part will be choosing which ones to pursue to ensure that you give people what they never even dreamed of.

Coming up with Surprise is not for managers of ISO 9001 companies, who probably have to check an 853-page manual and fill out forms in triplicate just to see if they have permission to pick up this book. It's for the renegades, the adventurous, the entrepreneurs, be they out on their own or lucky enough to work in a progressive environment that gladly embraces the art of Surprise. This spirit is well-defined by a blogger known only as "Uncle Saul" (we all have one of those, I guess) on SocialTech.com, a Southern California high-tech insiders site, who said: "Entrepreneurs must define a series of skirmishes, they do not need to devise elaborate battle plans."[2]

And as you define your Surprising skirmishes, remember two things. First of all, don't be obnoxiously obtrusive, a caution carved in stone by an article in *Brandweek* that said: "If you're going to interrupt someone's day, make it worth his or her while. If your activity makes you feel icky, bored or even stupid, do consider whether passers-by will feel the same. A pissed-off customer is worse than no customer."[3] You may want to get in their face, but don't get on their nerves. A great lesson of doing one without the other is demonstrated by how the San Diego Humane Society and SPCA brought attention to their very important cause. On a five block radius surrounding the highly-trafficked Horton Plaza shopping center, the nonprofit group unleashed 120 mad dogs . . . well, life-sized cut-out images of them, at least. Each adorable pooch placard was emblazoned with a powerful message about animal cruelty, abuse, and adoption, which the rush hour foot and car circulation found hard to miss, but easy to avoid if they so wanted to.

The second thing to keep in mind is that Surprise is not yelling "Fire!" in a crowded theater. Surprise may be explosive, loud, and powerful, but there needs to be a finesse involved when crafting it. A caveat here for what you learned back in Chapter 5—garnering attention is great, but it has to be the right type of attention. If I walked through Times Square without my pants or underwear, I'd get attention alright, but not necessarily the type that would endear me to others and concretize my professional relationship with them. To explain by example what not to do, consider this promotional card I had mailed to me, shown (sorry, folks) in Figure 7.1.

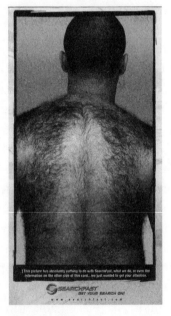

Figure 7.1

If your stomach is still churning and you managed to pass over the copy below the human rainforest, here's what you missed:

This picture has absolutely nothing to do with SearchFast, what we do, or even the information on the other side of this card . . . we just wanted to get your attention.

Well congrats, SearchFast. And now that you did, we know who to ignore the next time we hear their name. SearchFast combines the bad and the ugly rolled into one. The rest of this chapter outlines the good and the great, separates them by tactical themes, and provides an easy-to-grasp definition before diving headfirst into the deep ocean of glorious supporting examples for each one. One last thing to note: the tactics, while separated here for comprehension issues, are often shaken into a Surprise cocktail for maximum effect when actually put into play. They are not necessarily meant to be mutually exclusive, but as an exquisite blend, like Johnnie Walker Blue.

But leave the Johnnie Walker alone for now. Instead, go grab a coffee (or a Red Bull, or both). You need to stay alert. In the epic Chapter 7, we've got a lot of ground to cover.

Tactic 1: Wear Virgin Contact Lenses

We start off sweetly and innocently with an accoutrement that strips away our preconceived notions, eliminates our cynicism, and best of all, bashes through all the calloused blockades of "here's why we can't do this." Wearing Virgin Contact Lenses enables you to paradoxically see things again for the first time, and puts you in the frame of mind to recreate that sense of wonderment for your customers.

Directions are simple: insert, then look at your product, your service, your dilemma as if you've never seen it before. What "was" never was. Used properly, Virgin Contact Lenses show how things "could've been," and provide the entrée into an alternative universe where it now actually can be. Albert Einstein once said that you can never solve a problem in the framework in which it was created. If nothing else, Virgin Contact Lenses change the framework.

A simple example is how Kraft used Virgin Contact Lenses to breathe new life into its Nabisco cookie and snack product lines. Given the growing concern about health issues and rampant obesity, the company was looking for a way to avoid the vilifying of this multibillion-dollar slice of its pie. In an inspired vision, Kraft decided to shift focus away from the food itself, and onto the food's caloric content. The Pow! Moment resulted in a new form of packaging, the "100-Calorie Pack," which delivered the win-win of minimizing guilt and maximizing margins. Now consumers wouldn't be buying snacks *per se*, they'd be buying a small portion of their daily calorie intake, 100 calories of Chips Ahoy! or Ritz crackers or Planter's Peanuts or whatever (the product was less important than the number) at a time, and paying more on a per-calorie basis for it.

As win-wins go, this was a big one. During its introductory year of 2004, Kraft crowed that sales of 100-Calorie Packs "exceeded expectations," and the product was cited by CEO Roger Deromedi in Q1 of 2005 as one of the key factors that helped push the corporation to its first quarterly profit increase in nearly two years. Seeing this, other food companies, like Frito-Lay and Procter & Gamble, quickly jumped aboard the 100-Calorie scooter (a slimmed-down version of the standard bandwagon) with portioned-packs of household names like Doritos, Cheetos, Pringles, and minicans of Coke and Pepsi. A Surprising new industry was born.

Better still, the media jumped aboard with a most positive buzz. "For consumers, knowing what to eat and how much to eat is incredibly confusing, so having portion-controlled products helps," said Nick Hahn, a food industry strategist at Vivaldi Partners, in an *International Herald-Tribune* article. "I think you'll eventually see single-portion, calorie-control packages from everyone."[4] And as the fat-free icing on the 100-calorie cupcake, even the nutritionists were happy. Marion Nestle, an apt-named professor of nutrition at New York University, bubbled: "For people who feel deprived because they can't have cookies, I can see where this is a benefit. One-hundred calories of cookies is not anything that as a nutritionist I'm going to be the slightest bit upset about."[5] (I wonder how Marion would feel about the next wave, which saw a number of food companies, including the makers of Pup-Peroni Protein-Packed Dog Snacks, double-down with 50-calorie packs.)

The 100-calorie success story seemed to spawn a run on Virgin Contact Lenses throughout the food and drink biz. New York's Amazing Food Wine Co. took the guesswork out of wine/food pairing by branding its vintages in bottles brightly labeled "Wine That Loves Roasted Chicken" and "Wine That Loves Pizza" (much better names than the smartly-rejected "Roasted Chicken Wine" and "Pizza Wine," don't you think?). Pizza itself took on a new form. The Florida-based Fusion Pizza chain made a big deal about organic ingredients and its environmentally-friendly operations, but it was the unexpected long, rectangular shape of its pies that got people talking. Then pizza was made like ice cream and plopped into cones. Europe's Konopizza today competes with L.A.'s Crispy Cones for "I thought of it first" bragging rights, but Crispy Cones' founder, Nir Adar, has the best quote about the hot, gooey, portable concoction: "Cone pizza will be the iPod of food."[6]

My favorite edible example of all, however, is how Post Cereals updated and relaunched its venerable Shreddies brand without changing a thing—well, almost. A well-known breakfast table staple for close to 70 years in Great Britain, Canada, and New Zealand, Shreddies was "reintroduced" last year as Diamond Shreddies. The illustration shown in Figure 7.2 says it all.

Figure 7.2 One small turn for a cereal, one giant twist for mankind.

Simple, hysterical, effective—great Pow! The idea was the brainchild of Hunter Somerville, a 26-year-old intern at the Ogilvy & Mather agency, who is still somewhat embarrassed by it. While the agency powers-that-be were holed up trying to brainstorm a new direction for the tired brand, Somerville was kicking around some silly concepts for the back of the box. "I figured if I can't write the big idea, I might as well make them laugh," explained the one-time improv comedian. "I thought it was the stupidest, worst idea ever."

Perhaps, but wearing Virgin Contact Lenses blurs that all-too-solid line between foolishness and brilliance. The company has since exploited this simple 45-degree turn to the max, including a promotion with actual diamonds as prizes and a web site that features some delightfully funny, real focus group sessions (well, the people are real; the moderator is faux and in on the joke) where perplexed interviewees reflect on the exciting innovation of a "whole new level of geometric superiority" and admit that the Diamond Shreddie has "more punch" to its taste than its blander square predecessor. Once again, the media tossed laurels. *Maclean's,* Canada's weekly national news magazine, gushed:

> *By tilting an old product on its side, literally, it succeeded in tilting it afresh in consumers' imaginations as well. And in the process, it also skewered the hollow emperor's new clothes essence of "new and improved" product boasts and misplaced attempts to update classic brands. In such a landscape, the most radical change is, wait for it: no change at all.*

Some things did change radically, however. Somerville was hired full-time at the agency with a healthy raise. And the "worst" became the best, one of them at least, as the Diamond Shreddies campaign was shortlisted alongside eventual winners Halo 3 and Burger King for a gleaming, roaring Golden Lion at the 2008 Cannes Advertising Awards.

Okay, I'm full. Enough food—time for underwear. Sounds ridiculous, but to make a point, let me show you how Virgin Contact Lenses (let's call them VCLs for short from now on) can be used to create Surprise anywhere. Late last summer, I helped an entrepreneurial neighbor named Asher Adler get an underwear business off the ground by popping a pair of VCLs into his eyes. His original concept was to concentrate on the design, and stand out via the use of color and pattern.

"Done to death," I told him. "From ultra-premium like D&G to department store brands like Calvin Klein, they're all doing it. You don't stand a chance."

His back-up plan: Underwear with a hidden pocket for a condom.

"Oy," I grimaced. "Novelty store only. Lifespan of a tse-tse fly."

Then we got down to business trying to find the secret to selling stuff that is still purchased for most men by their significant others. We went to my underwear drawer and looked inside. About three dozen pairs of 'em. All types, and nothing incredible.

"I expected more from you," Asher said. "You're the most fashionable guy I know, and you don't seem to care."

"That's just the point," I admitted. "As long as they're comfy. In fact, I've had some of these for close to a decade. But who knows that?"

That's when it hit us. A new way to sell underwear—to men, and especially to the women who buy underwear for them. It's not about the aesthetics, or even the fit. If a fashion-conscious guy like me has skivvies about to celebrate their tenth birthday, then I have to be prompted, shamed even, into buying anew.

The solution: a date. Not a "Best By" date like you'd see on milk or medicines, but a "Made Fresh On" date like you'd see on beer or potato chips. Asher's underwear line wouldn't be a fashion item, rather a time-sensitive personal hygiene item. And it would be called "Spanking New."

So this scenario is for the guys out there: Imagine if your boxers were emblazoned with, "Made Spanking New on March 5, 2009." Two years from now, no matter how well they've been preserved, will you *really* be comfortable pulling them on? Worse yet, what will your wife or girlfriend say? Trust me, their "Spanking New" date tolerance will be way less than yours.

Like the 100-Calorie Packs, eventually everybody will get into the act. Perhaps the "Spanking New Date" will become an industry standard. But by looking at underwear through VCLs, at least Asher's idea has a chance to get off the ground, to delight buyers in department stores and boutiques looking for something new. (And I bet that if you haven't already done so, you'll be rummaging through your underwear drawer sometime soon . . . just to see.)

Another powerful case for VCLs is a corporate video I like to screen in my seminars on Surprise. It never fails to elicit row upon row of classic Surprise faces (although by describing the video here, I'm sacrificing its Pow! at future events. Oh well . . .). The ingenious little film comes from a German energy company called EPURON GmbH, a subsidiary of Conergy AG, and its agency Nordpol+ Hamburg. In it, a menacing, lanky, oversized antagonist, dressed all in black but wearing an out-of-character, too-small bowler hat, basically intimidates, bullies, and bothers a whole series of people—he messes up a woman's hair, hikes up another one's skirt, blows sand in little girl's face, overturns a tent at an outdoor affair, even drops a flower pot from an apartment building balcony, narrowly missing two old ladies walking below. What makes him even more unlikable is his thick French accent and Gallic arrogance; in a voiceover interview, the nasty SOB has the nerve to lament his loneliness and complain how he is misunderstood.

Only at the film's end, when, instead of being shunned, his mischievous act of ruffling a man's newspaper is embraced and rewarded with a business card, do things start to make sense. "Somebody finally accepted me for what I am," the guy says. "I finally feel useful." You're still bewildered, until the kicker fades onto the screen.

Two words: "The Wind."

The film ends as our hero (everyone goes "Awwww" once they discover who he really is) turns around and spins a scale model of a windmill turbine that has been sitting behind him, in full view, the whole time. Two minutes and four seconds of brilliance, and yes, yet another Cannes Golden Lion winner.

Virgin Contact Lenses are a magnificent tool. They change perspective. Suddenly, that coffee cup you accidentally left on top of your car as you drove off becomes a magnetic interactive promo campaign for Starbucks (for seven days in 2006, the company gave out close to 20,000 Surprise gift cards to people who were Good Samaritan enough to intervene and point out the potential spill hazard). Suddenly, that car you're trying to sell to younger drivers becomes a sound system with wheels (ads for the 2007 Dodge Caliber *Play* Edition trumpeted its 9 speakers, 458 watts, Boston Acoustic speakers and subwoofer, Sirius Satellite Radio with 12-month subscription, and basically nothing else). Suddenly, that breast cancer awareness web site that is trying to reach both young women and men becomes a coy come-on (the charitable organization Rethink Breast Cancer put up posters of a woman barely covering up with the headline "Check Out My Breasts.com").

Suddenly, it's a new world—for you. And for those you are trying to reach.

Tactic 2: Shock and AHH...

Now that we're done with the sweetest of tactics, it's time to take our virgin eyes for a walk on the wild side. If an ultimate goal of Surprise is to spark Euphoric Shock, this tactic sacrifices some of the euphoria for the sake of making a more pointed point. Shock and Ahh . . . does exactly that: it penetrates senses swiftly and deftly, opens eyes, mouths and minds, and then settles the message's recipient down with a feeling of "Oh, I get it" relief. In physical terms, it's like a slap in the face immediately followed by a hug. The most important factor in using the Shock and Ahh . . . tactic to instigate Surprise is the combination of speed and strength; a strong message delivered too slowly will have diminished effect, as will a swiftly delivered weak message.

Ken Rossignol, the editor of Maryland's *St. Mary's Today* newspaper, found an optimum balance between fast and furious last Christmas. Rossignol's brother was regrettably killed by a drunk driver in 1975, and in his brother's honor, the ballsy editor put together a simple yet breakthrough promotion in his paper. He offered a "Free Coffin Giveaway" to the first drunk driver to die "during this holiday drinking and driving season!" The announcement was illustrated by a coffin and martini glass, and went on to say:

> *Tired of all the nagging of loved ones, stupid commercials from MADD, cops, judges and addiction counsellors? Throw a final bender this Christmas and get a cheaper funeral by being the ST. MARY'S TODAY Christmas Party DWI Dead Driver Winner! We will throw in a FREE wooden coffin . . . however, you could just call a cab and save us the pile of scrap lumber.*[7]

Unconventional and a little on the edge, but this gets the point across with a gulp. While, sadly, the odds point to someone actually taking Ken up on his offer, I can guarantee that this approach narrowed the pool from which he chose his "winner."

As raw as Rossignol comes across, he pales in comparison to a campaign put together by Canada's Workplace Safety & Insurance Board. To drive home the message that all accidents are in fact preventable, the Board sponsored a series of TV and print ads that featured horrific visuals more at home in gross-out flicks like *Hostel* or *Saw.* One TV spot showed a sous-chef slipping in a restaurant kitchen and being scalded—quite yuckily and graphically so, I might add—by a pot of boiling oil. Print ads were equally as shocking, including the one that may make you queasy in Figure 7.3, where a "Danger" sign severs a machine operator's left arm.

Figure 7.3 Good thing he was wearing those safety goggles . . .

This approach may not be everyone's cup of tea (or bucket of blood, perhaps), but I assure you that these ads did not go unnoticed. In fact, even though the TV spots were only shown after 8:00 P.m. to reach a more mature audience, the public reacted loudly; half of them in catatonic horror, the other half in hearty applause that someone had the guts to tell it—and show it!—like it really is.

Despite its name, not every Shock and Ahh . . . Surprise is one of life-and-death consequences. There is a more light-hearted use of the tactic, like the ones I suggested to Douglas Mandel, a designer and retailer of understated, high-end menswear, whose boutique had been burglarized three times (!!!) in six months, to the tune of $120,000 in losses. "You've got to be doing something very right," I tried to console him, "if crooks are triple-risking arrest just to steal your clothes."

Instead of wallowing in pity or packing it in, Douglas' first move was to send customers an e-mail announcing the cheekily-titled "It's a Steal" sale, where he cleared out his remaining merchandise to start anew. Great start, but there's a way to overshoot the lemonade and turn these lemons into vintage limoncello. How about:

- If Douglas fully exploited his suffering and labels himself "The *TRUE* Fashion Victim."

- If he flanked his doors with Fort Knox-like sentries and overnight armed guards? Yes, it may be costly, but perhaps not as much as three break-ins and increased insurance premiums. "Establish a distinctive high-security look and you'll get media coverage around the world," I told him. "Then dare the crooks to hit you again."

- If he set up a mail-order business and delivered each piece in a lock-box that wailed like a burglar alarm when opened. For really big orders, skip FedEx or UPS and have them delivered by Brinks or Wells Fargo.

❦ If he offered a reward of a year's wardrobe to anyone who can provide info that leads to the arrest of the SOBs that robbed him ... and then offer to design prison uniforms for the perpetrators once they're caught.

❦ If he stages his next fashion show in a jail. (Hey, something similar worked for Johnny Cash!)

Foolish? On one level, yes. But way more effective and talk-worthy than a 30 percent-off sale, or something equally benign, expected, and ignored.

Great Shock and Ahh ... tactics are unignorable. Like a bee sting, they're in and out before you know what hit you. It can work with visuals, like this New Zealand TV announcement for the TV debut of the Quentin Tarantino film *Kill Bill*, shown in Figure 7.4.

Figure 7.4   Sponsored by a TV Network ... and a car wash.

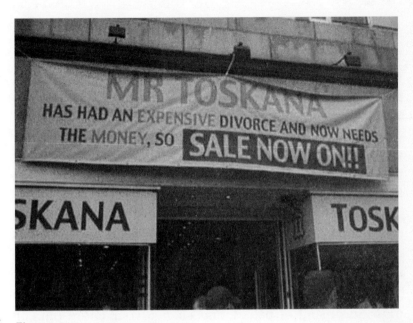

Figure 7.5   Telling it like it is.

Or it can work with words alone, like with the retailer shown in Figure 7.5.

Taking this concept down one level further, even mere letters, when jumbled in order, can provide a sizable jolt. Ask Trevor Beattie, the bad boy of British advertising, who saw the initials of his United Kingdom-based fashion client French Connection on a fax and decided to use them as a rebranding device. His breakthrough icon? "FCUK." (Note to stunned dyslexics: calm down, it's just a simple acronym for French Connection UK.) Campaigns with in-your-face slogans like "FCUK Fashion" helped to propel the brand, albeit scandalously, to over $100 million in annual sales in North America.

Whether you agree with Shock and Ahh . . . tactics or not is debatable. But then again, isn't that just the point?

Tactic 3: Words Are Important

Coincidence or serendipity? Tactic 3 is closely related to Theory three ("Little Things Mean A Lot") and is perhaps the most underrated implement in carrying it out. If Surprise is an explosion, a mere word can be the blasting cap that sets it off. In the whirlwind world of Surprise, words are frequently given the short shrift, underdogged in comparison to bombastic visual or audio effects. But ask any contract lawyer, hostage negotiator, or veteran Surprise marketer—the difference between brouhaha and disregard, between devotion and misunderstanding, is often dependent on the addition, subtraction, or modification of just one of these little buggers. So choose yours wisely.

Great verbiage can sneak up on you and appear in the most Surprising of places, and change your entire opinion about a product or service in the process. For instance, this is what appeared in the fine print dead zone of mobile service provider Helio's print ads in 2007:

> *Don't blame us for third-party content or services. Our super-advanced 3G service is available in select locations in the red states, the blue states and even the green states. Service is subject to Helio's Membership Terms. Some restrictions apply, but not too many. See your Helio representative for the few that do. Helio, the Helio logo, Ocean and 'Don't Call It a Phone' are trademarks of Helio LLC. For more information, on Helio, visit www.helio.com. And congrats, you're the only person who's made it this far.*

In the song "Step Right Up," Tom Waits cackles the words: "You got it, buddy—the large print giveth, and the small print taketh away." But even though it's printed in near-invisible, four-point, wispy grey type, Helio's small print giveth a lot of entertainment, it giveth a few smiles, and most importantly, it giveth a lot of insight into the company's image and spirit. It's cheeky, revealing, and actually a whole lot more fun than most wireless carriers' actual in-ad copy. Fine print doesn't have to be boring legalese. It's a zone where few people ever really venture, which makes it fine territory for planting Surprise mines.

Or check out this excerpt from the back of the box of Merrick's Spring Fling:

> *Our Spring Fling is a delightful tryst of the senses that pairs a lover of fine foods with an innocent bystander such as our gourmet can entrées and whirls them off into wedded bliss. At Merrick, we're suckers for the whole romance thing; maybe it's because we were the last ones asked to the spring dance or were never voted cutest couple. Whatever the method is that helped shape our soft spot, we are committed to love. So pack up the red gingham check blanket, a couple of champagne flutes, a lite lunch in your trusty old wooden picnic basket your mom gave you and let's head to the park.*

Paints quite the picture doesn't it? Oh, I almost forgot to mention . . . Spring Fling is a six-pack sampler of dog food. Woof, woof.

Maybe the people responsible for the Merrick Spring Fling had something to do with the following. As a dog owner myself, I know that there are two types of us: those who pick up after their dogs, and those who don't give a . . . well, uh, you know what I mean. If you are the former, you don't need a sign to tell you what to do. And if you're the latter, you'll disregard them no matter what they say. Unless, of course, they're as clever as the ones put up by the District of North Vancouver, shown in Figure 7.6.

Figure 7.6   Bilingualism at its best.

Once again, simple, impossible to ignore, and well worth a MilkBone, don't you think? A mere 17 words, or 14 and three sound effects, that lead to a few thousand conversations.

The right words can perform the magic act of transforming a common tangible into an exceptional intangible, like a mere menu item that will get tongues a-wagging in more ways than one. Take this tale of two different hamburgers, or shall I say, take these hamburgers that have become two different tales being told.

The most expensive bun and patty combo in America can be found in Colorado's Chophouse Restaurants. At $275 each, the "Dom Perignon Chophouse Burger" more than doubles the mega-price of its competition (the burger at Boca Raton's Old Homestead for $125 or the $99 one at New York's DB Bistro Moderne are pricey enough), yet the real story is not on your taste buds, but on the menu, which reads:

Chophouse Burger and Dom Perignon

Served with French Fries

10 oz. certified Angus Beef

$275

Without the Dom Perignon

$15

Not only is this a chat-inducer, but a rare specimen of a sense of humor in a high-end restaurant, adding to the element of Surprise.

Then there's what I call "The Last Supper," over at the notorious Heart Attack Grill in Phoenix, Arizona. The unconventional naming convention of its menu, like the 8,000-calorie hunka-hunka burning love called the "Quadruple Bypass Burger" and its accompanying "Flatliner Fries" ("Deep fried in pure lard!" boasts its web site), along with the hottie waitresses dressed as nurses that serve it all up, have made this a tourist destination . . . albeit for unhealthy tourists. The joint's slogan? "Taste Worth Dying For." Crass, but effective. Name me a burger joint in your town that has drawn TV crews from as far as Germany, Japan, France, and of course, Fox News.

Words can change everything, everywhere. Attitudes, perceptions, moods, purchase decisions—they're all susceptible to how you play with the 26 letters and handful of punctuation at your fingertips. A company I incessantly use to illustrate this point is woot.com. If you don't know Woot yet, you should. It's one of the great sites on the web, period. Woot is an ecommerce destination that sells one tech product—just one!—every day, but does so with words completely spectrum-opposite of the usual dull jargon that curses most other sites that sell stuff. Whoever writes the copy is a maestro, pixie-dusting even the most mundane piece of plastic, wires, and silicon with a sales job so symphonic, you must have it . . . even though you probably don't need it. (Offshoot sites Wine.Woot and the Threadless quasi-clone Shirt.Woot are equally as good.) Compare Woot's daily writing—entertainment in its own right—to the usual cliché-ridden, committee-vetted sludge that infests most commercial sites and documents and you'll get the gist of why words are important.

Don't let Woot intimidate or derail you. A misconception about Tactic three is that since it relies on words, you have to be a poet, a scribe, or a wordsmith to take advantage of it—not so. It's imagination that drives this tactic, not vocabulary or a thesaurus (although proficiency in use of either won't hurt). Even one well-placed word can make the difference between boredom and brilliance, as I discovered while peering into two very different store windows.

The first was in Florence, Italy at Vilebrequin, a purveyor of high-priced, luxury bathing suits for men. Instead of the standard "Closed" sign, the Vilebrequin store chose the more colorful, bespoke term, "Gone Tanning" to notify customers of its after-hours status. Frankly, I always felt a "Closed" sign in a window sends a bummer of a message. Put another way, you've got trouble if your walk-up customers have to wonder if you're open, and there has to be a way to continue communicating your message when you're not . . . like the one brought to my attention by German-based British ex-pat blogger Adam Lawrence that went:

> *Sorry, we're out of town selling at the fair.*
> *BUT our webshop is open, and there's an internet café right behind you.*
> *Mike will give you a free coffee if you mention this sign.*

The second one-word wonder was spotted in Vancouver (given the aforementioned dog story, this town is obviously a hotbed of brilliant sign-writers), at the Mui Garden Restaurant, which posted this boast in its storefront:

OUR CURRY IS PROBABLY THE BEST IN THE WORLD.

Think about it—the statement "Our Curry Is the Best in the World" would be met with a "yeah right," ridiculed, and ultimately dismissed, particularly in Vancouver, which is not exactly renowned as the universal focal point of Indian cuisine. But the addition of the off-balancing adverb "probably," purposely not capitalized, makes what would be conceived as forgettable stupidity into a conversation-starter . . . and most "probably" a lure through the doors.

No hype, no outrageous claims that would be impossible to live up to, no claims of being The Best!, The Greatest!, or Number One! That's what makes this Vancouver curry horn-toot work. These days, cynicism and a shrewd marketplace have rendered overhype counterproductive, which may be why one of 2007's top best-sellers was a slim volume simply entitled, *On Bullshit*. We won't get fooled again.

A little truth, a dash of humility, the spice of a sense of humor—all of these go a long, long, way in making words important. Embody those traits and the words will flow. Words can be learned; character and personality are a tougher study.

All this reminds me of a telltale cartoon I still recall from a *MAD* magazine piece about, of all things, pizza. While published a half-century ago, it shows the power of truth, humility, humor, and the right words. In it, there are four pizza parlors situated next to each other. Each has a front-facing promotional sign. The first says, "Tony's: The Best Pizza Pies in the City." Another says, "Pascual's: The Best Pizza Pies in the Country." A third ups the ante and says, "Giuseppe's: The Best Pizza Pies in the World." Finally, above a restaurant far smaller and less elegant than the previous trio, is the sign that seals and delivers. It reads simply:

IRVING'S: THE BEST PIZZA PIES ON THE BLOCK.

Tactic 4: Rally Against Stereotypes

The inspiration for this tactic came on a very tiring day in 2006 when I gave speeches at three events. The speeches and locations were different, but the reaction was the same each time: "I didn't know you were a suit and tie guy!" For some reason, most people perceive me as a "jeans and t-shirt guy," so when I show up somewhere—anywhere, I guess—wearing a navy blue suit, a striped shirt, and contrasting op-art Duchamp tie, well ... Surprise! The reality, though, is that I have over 30 suits and over 100 ties in my closets. It's just that the Andy Nulman "stereotype" (or "Personal Brand" in the parlance of digital marketing guru Mitch Joel) is anything but formal.

My learning in all this is that in the quest for Surprise, stereotypes are your best and most reliable friend. They're the lob ball that makes it easy to really hit one out of the park. And they're everywhere. When a TV actor spends her summer in a Broadway musical, the reaction is usually "I never knew she could sing!" When the quiet brainy kid at the back of physics class stars for the school basketball team, you'll inevitably hear "I never knew he was an athlete!" This is why there's also such incredible fascination over cheesy TV shows like *Dancing with the Stars,* which takes well-known names out of their commonly-known comfort zone. People like to put others into boxes. When we break out of them—***Boinnnng!***—it's like the proverbial showgirl popping out of the birthday cake.

I use people as an example, but the same goes for products, stores, companies, ideals—preconceived notions about 'em lead to deep-rooted stereotypes; stereotypes you can easily break, reverse, and exploit. As tactics go then, four is perhaps the easiest one to carry out:

1. Find your inner stereotype.

2. Head in the opposite direction.

3. Then watch for the gasps.

In an utopian world, perhaps this tactic would help us counter racial ignorance. Get a bigot to spend some quality time with a minority they have long pigeonholed and let them be shocked by the reality: "Geez, I always thought you (*insert name of minority here*) guys were (*insert foolish stereotype here*)."

Well, I can dream, can't I? Until then, we will have to be content with these more corporate examples of using stereotypes to Surprise by playing against them.

Clothes are great stereotypical starting points to divert from. I remember the first time I saw both Doug Hall and Loretta LaRoche speak. Doug was one of the keynote speakers at a gathering of Top 40 Under 40 business leaders I had the privilege to be among. Barefoot and sporting a loud Hawaiian shirt, he came across as the hapless Christian in a den of sharp, rapacious, type-A lions. Tiny little Loretta, wearing a feather boa and Viking horns, took to the stage as part of a multispeaker Motivation Day in front of 4,500 professionals who paid up to $1,500 apiece to be there (other people on the bill that day included a big Bill named Clinton, cyclist and cancer activist Lance Armstrong, and legendary Hollywood producer Peter Guber). Both times, as Loretta and Doug took to the mic, I winced, thinking that these poor souls were about to be eaten alive. Both times I was dead wrong, as the lowering of expectations and emergence from "left field" saw both Doug and Loretta overshadow the competition and conquer the crowd. I'll never forget the scene of some of the corporate world's most powerful and hardened execs holding hands (!!) and singing along with Loretta to Dean Martin's "That's Amore."

Now on to the bastion of western capitalism, Wall Street. Think of those who work there, particularly investment bank analysts, and you conjure up the vision of blue suits, striped shirts, and ties . . . sort of like me on that fateful tri-speech day. By nature, Wall Streeters are conservative, careful with words; not just going with the grain, but separating it into equidistant rows and columns. So no wonder a very accurate sell-aide analyst from Lazard Capital Markets named Joel

Sendek generates such a commotion. Joel's day job is research-ing biotech companies, making calls whether investors in this roller-coaster risky sector should buy, sell, or hold their posi-tions. But his research report voicemail calls have become legendary, as he delivers them as full-fledged poems, or more recently, as songs, parodying classic tunes from Don McLean, Louis Armstrong, The Stones, and Bruce Springsteen (*Fortune* magazine called him "The Weird Al of Wall Street"). As one client admitted: "You get so many voicemails, and they all say the same thing. His are a nice, goofy ray of hope in a legion of doom."[8]

Sendek shows that occupations are equally as useful as stereotype set-ups to rebel against. At the Retail Advertising Council Conference in Chicago, I ran into two companies that blow open their respective industries' pigeonholes with a wrecking ball.

The first is called Accessvia, a printer that provides in-store signage and desktop publishing apps to the retail trade. Score, right? Wrong. At the RAC show, these guys had:

- The best booth giveaways, including a coloring book that was the best sales-message-disguised-as-entertainment that I've seen in ages (see Figure 7.7).

- The best in-booth promos; two in fact—a coloring con-test and photo shoot.

- The best logo, many of them actually, all featuring the company's black cat mascot.

- The best slogan: "The Eternal Order of Accessvia."

- The coolest CEO, Dean A. Sleeper, a.k.a. the Richard Branson of printing.

- The best use-of-funds: sponsoring *Made to Stick* author Dan Heath's keynote and book-signing.

- The best stunt: an Airborne-reminiscent dollar bill blast to drive home their message that if you work with them, "money will fall from the sky."

Figure 7.7 The great Accessvia Coloring Book.

All this from an "old school" industry renowned for not being renowned. Despite this, Accessvia still wasn't the most outrageous sultan of shock at the conference. That honor went to a tiny Portland, Oregon company called Voodoo Doughnuts, who have generated a tidal wave of media buzz by doing to doughnuts what Cirque du Soleil did to the circus.

Voodoo Doughnuts sure ain't your father's Dunkin' Donuts or Krispy Kreme. In addition to live concerts, legal weddings, and real Swahili lessons in its one and only store (which is open 24 hours a day, every day of the year), Voodoo Doughnuts also offers some infamous X-rated competitions, like the Annual Cockfest, where men gather to stack doughnuts on their . . . well, uh . . . At the RAC conference, stylish cofounders Kenneth "Cat Daddy" Pogson and Tres Shannon threw down their renowned "Tex-Ass Challenge," where contestants had to wolf down a super-sized doughnut, the equivalent of a half-dozen regular treats, in less than 90 seconds.

The wildness carries onto Voodoo Doughnuts' all-made-by-hand menu as well. My faves include an actual Voodoo Doll doughnut (which "bleeds" raspberry jam when jabbed with pretzel-stick "pins" [Ooh, gross! See Figure 7.8]) and a Bacon-Maple Bar complete with real bacon strips. Compare that to the ordinary, assembly-line doughnut shops that line

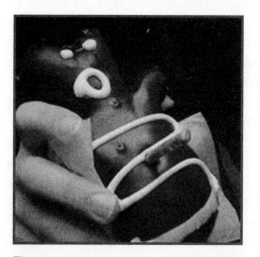

Figure 7.8 For the sweet-toothed sadist in all of us.

strip malls and food courts across the country. By the way, they taste good, too.

A little warning though; use Tactic 4 with some discretion. This stereotype-smashing tactic is so easy to carry out, sometimes the gasps it can provoke may be a little too loud for some ears. This I found out firsthand a couple of years ago, when the elders at my synagogue contacted me to help them out on their annual Cantorial concert. For those of you not familiar with the concept, traditional Cantorials are filled with traditional religious songs sung by traditional Cantors, hence the name (been done the same way for centuries).

Obviously, I was called upon to do something different. My concept was a quasi-blasphemous twisting of the concert called—wait for it—***Cantorama!***

While it would indeed feature many of the standard religious songs, they would be sped up some and played by a whup-ass rock band. Since most Cantors are blessed with versatile, booming voices, the plan was to also have them sing pop standards and show tunes, but backed by the congregation's choir, with some of the modern musical arrangements changed to a Jewish/Klezmer sound, including heritage Jewish instruments. All in all, the goal was to turn the concept upside down.

Well, the Cantors loved it. "Cantorama!" gave them a chance to stretch their wings, their vocal chords, and have a bit of fun. But the people who had to lead the orchestra, sell the tickets, and face the congregants were aghast.

"Over my dead body!" many said. And given the intensity of the Talmudic debate that my concept incited, it almost came to that. Basically, "Cantorama!" only got as far as my head . . . and the poster mock-up shown in Figure 7.9. Perhaps I took the term "High Holidays" a little too literally.

Figure 7.9   Sacrelgious maybe,
but it would've sold tickets.

Tactic 5: Look In The Rearview Mirror

I'm no Alfred Eisenstaedt, but one of the best photos I ever took was on Daytona Beach about 25 years ago, when I was still a student. It was the break of day. I parked my car on the beach and shot the view through my front windshield. The photo, which I have since lost, showed a dusky day ahead illuminated by the sunrise captured in my rearview mirror.

A little overly poetic, but it is that vantage point that defines the method behind Tactic five. By looking, and doing things, backwards, you may stumble upon the idea that can drive the future.

At the root of The Rearview Mirror is simple reverse psychology. I've always said that the best way to get someone to pass something along—a message, an email, an invitation—is to say **"Please, please, *please* keep this to yourself!"** While we are, for the most part, honest, law-abiding citizens, deep down there's that seed of larceny that makes us enjoy the feeling of being counterintuitive.

I can't think of a better case in point than the Reverse Shoplifting operation I helped institute for a blogging buddy, author Dan Ward (a payback for sending me the Bounce Fabric Softener card mentioned in Chapter 6, I suppose). Dan asked if I had any cool, inexpensive but effective ways to spread the word about his book, *The Simplicity Cycle.* He bemoaned the fact that in a world of Stephen Kings, J.K. Rowlings, and Malcolm Gladwells, what chance did an independently published military man like himself have?

For some reason, I thought of the taunting title of Abbie Hoffman's 1960s counterculture manifesto, *Steal This Book,* and then the Reverse Shoplifting idea just flowed into my head. My emailed advice to Dan said this:

> *How many hard copies do you have? Take a bunch, put a sticker on them saying something like **"Here's an incredible offer. Take this book home. IT'S FREE!!"** and sneakily leave them in the business sections of big bookstores. Inside, include a note that asks them to read it, pass it along, talk about it, blog about it if they are a blogger. This will create buzz, perhaps even scandal, but lemme tell you, it will spread the word.*

At first he was a little worried. "What if someone gets caught?" Dan asked. "Gets caught doing what?" I replied. "What's the punishment for leaving a book in a bookstore, or taking one with no ISBN (identifying) number that doesn't even belong to them? Frankly, for your sake, I'd pray for someone getting caught!"

Well, give Dan credit. He has cannonball cojones, and decided to take the plunge. He summoned up a commando team of equally daring friends who have snuck into bookstores in England, New York, L.A., Las Vegas, and Washington, D.C. to plant Dan's giveaways. I myself did the deed at airport bookstores in Boston, Chicago, and San Francisco; it was a blast! And while he hasn't broken through to the New York Times best-seller list, Dan has heard from newfound readers and fans all over the world.

The same type of backwards thinking saw the Bear Naked Granola company of Norwalk, Connecticut reverse-engineer the concept of trick-or-treating and pull off what I consider to be one of the best Halloween sales promotions of all time. While the food industry's big boys stocked supermarket and convenience store end-caps with stacks of chips, candies, and other junk food, Bear Naked recruited college student street teams across the country, outfitted them in red afro wigs and Bear Naked t-shirts, and went door-to-door to *GIVE AWAY* hundreds of thousands of granola samples.

Door-to-door marketing used to be a familiar, homespun North American staple (some of you older readers may remember "Avon calling!" and the Fuller Brush man), but with modern-day innovations like e-commerce and home invasions, having someone try to sell you something at your doorstep has kind of fallen out of favor.

Bear Naked's marketing director, Ryan Therriault, admitted that going door-to-door "is looked down upon," but said that "Halloween was the one day of the year that people would actually be expecting someone to show up at their door," which makes Bear Naked's reverse initiative even more

timely, ingenious, and Surprising. (Coming up next—Bear
Naked's Christmas promotion, where Santa takes presents
and slides *up* the chimney, and its Easter program, where the
Easter Bunny *picks up* chocolate eggs.)

Another brilliant Rearview initiative was put into play by
Montreal's McCord Museum. Without a blockbuster attraction, museums are a tough sell these days; I can recall a
study that revealed that one of the main draws for a modern museum is its café. That's a tough pill to swallow, but you
have to fill the halls somehow; hence the McCord's unapolo-
getic Fair-Weather Friends campaign, which transforms the
museum from a house of culture into the world's most expensive umbrella.

In an obvious but daring coup, the McCord becomes a
refuge from inclement climes by cutting its entrance price in
half on rainy days (see Figure 7.10). No catches, no fine print,

Figure 7.10   The world's most expensive umbrella.

just a gutsy idea that didn't merely Surprise, but outraged, the stuffy museum establishment. Quite the feat; not even David Copperfield in his prime could convert a museum into an umbrella.

Smart marketers like Smirnoff and Xbox took advantage of British artist Paul Curtis' look in the Rearview Mirror. Curtis, under his *nom d'artiste* Moose, "selectively scrubs" the dirty, derelict city property like grimy tunnel walls and sidewalks around London and Leeds, and forms words, images, and brand logos with the clean parts (a more sophisticated version of fingering "Wash Me!" on the window of a dirty car, I suppose). Some call this "reverse graffiti," but Curtis prefers the terms "clean tagging" or "grime writing." "It's refacing, not defacing," he told the *New York Times.* "Restoring a surface to its original state. It's very temporary. It glows and twinkles, and then it fades away."[9]

Some people, like the Leeds City Council, were less than thrilled with Curtis's work, and pondered whether they could charge him with breaking the law. A city spokesperson was quoted in *The Guardian* newspaper saying: "Leeds residents want to live in clean and attractive neighbourhoods, and expect their streets to be free of graffiti and illegal advertising. We also view this kind of rogue advertising as environmental damage and will take strong action against any advertisers carrying out such campaigns without the relevant permission."[10] But what offense are they going to charge him with? Illegal cleaning?

For true cheekiness though, the Rearview notion was taken to its most literal extreme by *Adweek* editor Matthew Grimm, who proposed the introduction of a brand-new medium called, "Ass-vertising," which he dubbed "the seamless integration of marketing communications into the consumer lifestyle." To wit:

"Ass-vertising gets back to basics. Pure communication. It is an alternative medium where attentions drift naturally. Media placement would involve the finest, shapely, toned asses, male and female, in the local market, and the message would boil down to the most space-efficient information: '**Shrek 3**,' '**Do The Dew**,' or simply '**Eat at Joe's**'. Messages can vary by your degree of chutzpah. A directly representative approach may tender butt-copy like '**Ass by Trimspa**,' '**Miller Lite, Low on Carbs**,' or '**Bally's/Bowflex/Crunch Was Here**.'"[11]

Far-fetched? Check back with me in a few years, when Anheuser-Busch, now that it's owned by the more free-wheeling, liberal Europeans, unveils its new campaign: "This Butt's For You!"

Tactic 6: Time-Bombing

While there is a more genteel way of describing this very effective Surprise tactic—planting seeds that will bloom and blossom at some point in the future—I am more partial to a military/incendiary analogy due to its spy-like secrecy upfront and its explosiveness down the road. Successful Time-Bombing requires that nobody knows or sees what you are doing at the start, but if played right, everybody does in the end when your preset triggers detonate and spread Pow! far and wide. Take that, Chris Anderson! You've got the Long Tail, we've got the Long Fuse!

Okay, let's give peace a chance; Time-Bombing isn't inherently violent. I love how big-shot Hollywood producer Bryan Grazer purveys his Pow! An article in the *New York Times* outlined his efforts to ensure he is long remembered after he departs a private function. When attending a dinner or party,

Grazer will leave behind a small photo of himself in an inexpensive heart-shaped frame, and mix it up among his host's family photographs. Over the years, the article revealed, he has left behind such photos at the homes of movie executives, socialites, and even one in Fidel Castro's military compound.

Somewhat less subtle is how Craig Yoe handles his Time-Bombs. Craig is the owner and chief bonkbrain at YOE! Studio, an outlandish creative services outfit that brings "Creativity up the Wazoo!" to already-imaginative companies like Disney, Marvel, Hasbro, and Nickelodeon (he is also the author of the book *A Million Thanks,* which is just that—the words "Thank You" repeated one million times). A fixture at the annual Licensing Show in New York, Craig has long been lamenting—and rightfully so—how traditional and dull the once-wild show has become. Last year, perhaps influenced by Matthew Grimm's Ass-vertising model, he decided to do something about it. Here's a slightly edited version of an email he sent me:

Yo, Andy!
I love the Licensing Show and the great people who run it, but we've been talking about how to make it even more fun. OK, here's my Big Idea:

1. *First thing Tuesday morning come get your YOE! Studio Thong at our booth.*

2. *Scurry to the restroom and put it on—under your clothes.*

3. *At precisely 12 o'clock noon everyone is to stop what they are doing, drop trou and sing in*

unison (to the tune of "Ding Dong, the Witch Is Dead") the following lyrics:

Ding dong, show your thong, It feels so good, it can't be wrong. Ding dong, show the world your tho-o-n-n-n-g-g-g . . .

4. *Then at the conclusion of the song hug your neighbor, then un-drop your trou and continue on with the all-important task of being a licensee or a licensor. That's it! It's that simple.*

This will be SO COOL! Imagine, people from many different countries, people of different colors, different ages, different shapes, and sizes all united together singing and celebrating our "thong-ness." Being open, being free, not only dropping our trou, but dropping our pretensions, dropping our inhibitions, dropping our darn pride that keeps us apart. I'm getting all choked up just thinking about how wonderful this is going to be, as I am sure you are.

(See Figure 7.11 for a picture of this glorious, world-changing thong.)

Paramedics—and lawyers—were put on red alert. At noon, the YOE! Booth was surrounded by throngs of thongs. And almost everyone was delighted.

"Some companies spent over 100,000 bucks on their booths, but we were the ones people really remembered," said Craig. "Certainly, some people were, shall we say, displeased, but if you're not pissing off a few people, you're not doing your job."

Then I suppose that my business partner Garner Bornstein was just doing his job when he printed up dozens of customized golf balls to commemorate our Internet humor

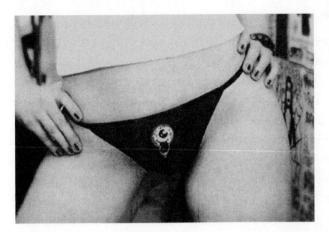

Figure 7.11   The infamous Yoe! Thong. Wear at your own risk.

portal[12] in 1999. Each ball showed our wicked mascot, the slip-of-the-tongue-named Fupp Duck, in the midst of a club-breaking fit, and was inscribed with these words:

IF FOUND
PLEASE CALL 514 289-9111
FOR REWARD

You can see both sides of the ball in Figures 7.12 and 7.13.

Figures 7.12 and 7.13   You'd figure the crazy duck would've telegraphed the joke, but no.

To this day, our receptionists still wield calls from anxious golfers chomping at the bit, wondering just what their mysterious reward will be. When told that it's all just a promotional joke to mark a (now long gone) comedy web site, most have a good laugh. Others do the Time-Bomb exploding for us. Oh well, as Craig says, if you're not . . .

One of the landmark events in Time-Bombing history took place in 1978, deviously implanted in CBS's embarrassingly cheesy *Star Wars Holiday Special.* While the show featured the film's cast and characters—alongside strikingly out-of-place guest stars like Bea Arthur, Harvey Korman, Art Carney, and the rock band Jefferson Starship—it also inexplicably tossed in an animated cartoon called "The Faithful Wookie," which introduced a previously unknown character named Boba Fett. During a commercial break, viewers were asked to send in a proof-of-purchase of any Star Wars action figure, and they would receive a Boba Fett.

"For kids who obsessed over every bit of the Star Wars universe, this mysterious character was electrifying," explained a *Fast Company* piece about the phenomenon. "It was the coolest toy to have. Two years later, when Boba Fett walked onto the screen of *The Empire Strikes Back,* the action-figure buyers got the ultimate payoff: So *this* is who Boba Fett was all along."[13]

Great Time-Bombs don't obliterate their targets; rather, they give them the opportunity to piece together the puzzle and involve themselves with the brand, product, or service. Call the consequence "Discoverability." For instance, for over a year, Reef, the beach lifestyle apparel company, marketed sandals that had a hidden bottle opener tucked inside the heel, but never advertised it or noted it in the packaging, preferring to let users discover the device by themselves and tell others. Edoc Laundry, the fashion company that boasts, "Our Clothes Tell Secrets," embeds clandestine codes into the design of their t-shirts; each one reveals part of a murder mystery that's played online, waiting to be solved by an Edoc Laundry customer. Even ol' faithful Levi's has jumped on the Bombwagon. A couple of years ago, I found a phone number discreetly penned among the buckshot holes, swirling tears, and tattoo-like inking of an extremely customized pair of jeans I bought from its flagship store in San Francisco. I assumed that it was the number to the store, but when I called it, it actually led me to a special Levi's Concierge Service, which invited me and three guests to a champagne-fueled, one-hour shopping experience.

Time-Bombs come in all shapes, sizes, and durations. They can range from a single, glow-in-the-dark ad for BMW's 1 Series on the front cover of *Vice* magazine that appears only when the lights are out, to a Condé Nast multimagazine MasterCard campaign that gives away priceless treasures, like original commissioned portraits by Julian Schnabel or around-the-world trips inside sealed, Oscar-like envelopes. They can pay off in a matter of minutes, like a secret prize taped to the bottom of a dinner plate at a fundraising event, or in a matter of months (or perhaps never), like the Dr. Pepper Guns 'n' Roses Challenge in March of 2008, when the soft drink company offered to "give a free can of Dr. Pepper to everyone in America (excluding ex-Guns members Slash and Buckethead)" if the band's forever-delayed *Chinese Democracy* album arrived any time during the calendar year (P.S. It did!). They take time to plan, and patience to pull off.

But when they hit, it's like the fourth of July. Stand back and enjoy the fireworks!

Tactic 7: Business Stupidity

I owe a lot to Roger von Oech on this one. His two afore-mentioned books taught me how to think differently long before Apple commandeered the expression for its ads. Over the years, I've played Whack-and-Kick-inspired mental games while bored in meetings, twisting the slogans and clichés I hear into an alternative universe. This led to the birth of Tactic 7, which was borne from a meeting where we decided that the key to our future was shoring up our "Business Intelligence." That got me to wondering what would happen, if instead, we shored up our "Business Stupidity," and did things that were so ridiculously wrong, they made everything right.

Seems that I'm not alone—"Business Stupidity" is widely used in Surprise marketing. Its put-into-play process is relatively elementary. Remember the Virgin Contact Lenses of Tactic 1? Well, find them and insert them once again . . . but this time, backwards. Forget the smart thing to do; twist logic and act like an idiot.

How else do you explain the actions of Internet shoe retail giant Zappos, which actually bribes its newest employees to quit by waving a $1,000 bill under their noses *(Stupid Idea: We Pay You To Leave)*. This offer, known rather ominously as "The Offer," comes during a month-long training period where prospective employees are instilled with the company's culture, vision, and profound obsession over dealing with its customers. The job isn't an easy one; in essence, Zappos is staffing a call center with personality that actually has to care about the people they're talking to.

After about a week of this detailed indoctrination, Zappos trots out "The Offer" in an effort to separate the golden nuggets from the silt. It sounds silly, but what it does is show who's willing to stay with the acute sense of commitment the company demands . . . and who won't be able to cut it. The "Leave Now" $1,000 may seem excessive, but it's peanuts compared to the cost of continued training and eventual replacement of the same employee. By the way, over 90 percent of prospective employees turn their backs on "The Offer" and decide to give their all to CEO Tony Hsieh and company. What's more, name me another company that has generated this much positive buzz and widespread kudos over an internal HR policy!

Staying on the subject of footwear, there's Blake Mycoskie's Tom's Shoes, which sends CFOs into convulsions by slashing its margin in half on every sale *(Stupid Idea: Cut Our Profit By 50 Percent)*. You see, for every pair of Tom's sold, the company *gives away* a corresponding pair to a needy child somewhere in the developing world (Blake started with Argentina, and has expanded the program into Africa). It's that simple—no fine print, no "portion of the proceeds," just a no-nonsense, bold, feel-good Pow! of a great marketing idea. In fact, calling it a marketing idea almost cheapens it; this "Buy One, Set One Free" may be the soul of a new way of doing business.

The folks at Jawbone electronics took this a step further. To cut through the thick human and media clutter that is the annual Consumer Electronics show in Las Vegas, the Bluetooth headset company orchestrated an audacious, no-questions-asked trade-in of one's current wireless phone earpiece for its brand-new one *(Stupid Idea: Give Away Our Product En Masse)*. No $20-off coupons, no mail-in rebates, just "gimme yours, here's ours." Over the giveaway period, Jawbone amassed barrels full of competitive products that obviously weren't doing the job, which not only stood as a convincing milestone of the trade-in's success, but heaped humiliation on every one of its competitors simultaneously and convincingly. I'm certain this cost Jawbone a bit more than handing out logo pens, mini-flashlights, or t-shirts, but the ensuing frenzy, snapped-and-blogged pictures (remember, this is a geek conference), and ecstatic word of mouth evangelists no doubt blew out the "R" in their ROI.

I don't know if this Business Stupidity is intentional, but it keeps me coming back to Mesquite, a Cajun restaurant near my house, for more. My favorite dish, the steamy Black Bean Soup, is *never* the same *(Stupid Idea: Be Inconsistent)*. Sometimes it's black, other times it's red, sometimes it comes with a couple of pieces of brisket floating inside, other times with a tortilla chip. The fact that I never really know which Black Bean Soup I'm getting is kind of irrelevant because no matter how it comes out, it's delicious and mouth-melting. Now I'm sure that Mesquite could put together some kind of standardized recipe and service manual to ensure the same thing every time around, but then they'd be like all the other restaurants. Their inconsistency is part of their charm.

A good starting point in exploiting Business Stupidity is reversing common sense. Take the following "tell me something I don't know" gem I once read in a marketing trade publication that went something like: Simply put, Americans either like to flaunt their thrift or wealth.

It made me laugh, because I had just lived through the two extremes. I was on a business trip that took me through Orlando, Florida and Aspen, Colorado. In the Sunshine State, I picked up a Ralph Lauren RRL jacket. What makes the jacket special is not just the intricate, obtuse patchworking, but the price; it had originally listed at $3,000, was marked down to $600, and I picked it up for 75 percent off that (that's $150 for those of you who are mathematically-challenged). This deal was *so* great, I still haven't removed the price tag from inside the jacket. It's become part of the story I tell each time someone comments on it. Most of the time, I even lift my arm to show the tag itself.

This got me to thinking that retailers should think of a way to "reverse-psychologize" the flaunting system. On the wealth side, we are happy to show off our designer names and logos loudly, but on the thrift side, the killer bargains remain stealthily anonymous ... unless you're a widemouth like yours truly *(Stupid Idea: Make Super-Sale Tags Highly Visible and Indestructible)*. Maybe "75% off" is the new Gucci.

Meanwhile, in Aspen, I visited a western wear store called Kemo Sabe. Unlike other luxury brands that melt your credit cards but do it with understated discretion, Kemo Sabe throws all tact out the window by flaunting the Yee-haw! Ridiculousness of their prices *(Stupid Idea: Goad People Into Overspending)* with slogans like:

"Calling All Cowboys With 10-Gallon Wallets C-notes Burnin' a Hole in Your Chaps? Don't Worry Pardner, We're Here to Help"

You may need two 10-gallon wallets at this place. A pair of boots can set you back over $4,000. Hat bands alone range up to $275. A couple of years ago in Vail, my kids saw a belt buckle they liked. "It's only $21.95, Dad!" they said. "That's reasonable," I thought, until I realized that the decimal point came after the five, and not before the nine. Yet the store thrives. Everything about what they sell is loud. Perhaps my Visible/Indestructible Tag idea would work here, too, but in reverse.

If you find that flaunting distasteful, just wait for the next three examples. Convenience store owners Couche-Tard, the

parent company of the Circle K chain, with over 2,100 locations across the United States and over $5 billion in annual
revenue, have embraced grossness as a naming strategy for
their teen-oriented "Froster" slush drinks *(Stupid Idea: Disgust Your Customers)*. Now, consumers with brave stomachs
can cool down with flavors like "Dirty Melted Snow," "Windshield Washer," or "Bloody Zit" and cap them off with crunchy
toppings like "Pus Powder," "Oily Blackheads," "Dried Scabs,"
and "Flesh Eating Bacteria." Yum—what's for dessert?

Over in St. John's, Newfoundland, tiny specialty retailer
The Bead Addict hand-delivered samples of their product to
artsy neighborhoods in pill bottles, miniature liquor bottles,
and syringes, each labeled, "For refills, visit The Bead Addict."
(Stupid Idea: Exploit a Social Weakness.)

And then there's the Italian jean brand named Nudie, and
its Slim Jim Dry Organic Denim. To get the optimum look,
Nudie says *NOT TO WASH* these jeans for a minimum of six
months *(Stupid Idea: Wear Dirty Clothes)*. Now I know this
sounds loopy, but there's a method to the madness. According
to the book that comes tucked into the pocket of each dry
jean, written in magnificent Italian English:

> *Real denim lovers use their jeans dry and we
> promise you a great result on the naturally worn
> denim. If you wait at least six months before wash-
> ing and use them a lot they will get fabulous.
> The indigo will be worn off the jeans in places
> where you make natural creases. When you finally
> wash your well-worn jeans, the indigo will fade off
> and you will get contrasts in those places. If you wash
> your dry denim after just a short period you will
> get a basic pair of navy blue jeans, which is quite*

boring actually. You have then started the magic bleeding process too soon and the possibility to get the marvellous contrast increases is gone.

In a world where most every premium jean looks about the same, Nudie is differentiating itself not by the look, but by the story . . . and maybe even by the smell. Since I bought mine, I've just had to tell people all about them. And people I've run into since telling the story stare at whatever jeans I'm wearing and ask, "Are those the ones you're not supposed to wash?" May not be great hygiene, but it's great marketing.

Business Stupidity is not just about the loud, the crass, or the gross. Sometimes it's about the serene and the serious . . . acting loud, crass, and gross. It's a bit of a stretch, but to close off Tactic 7, I bring you lululemon athletica, the much admired yoga/healthy lifestyle apparel retailer. To many, lululemon's pristine reputation is one of granola covered in karma and om; its mission statement says it is "Creating components for people to live a longer, healthier, more fun life," while its vision is an even more flowery "to elevate the world from mediocrity to a place of greatness."

So it came as a megavolt shock for lululemon's fanatic faithful to see the company introduce products such as "l'odeur, the world's first internal cologne," where "you eat the cologne pill and sweat the fragrance" (the accompanying video ad featured the line, "I will sweat like a fat man in a snowsuit, stuck in his car in the desert with his seat-heater on," and a shot of a man's underarm spraying a firehose of perspiration at his female companion), and the "Mansy," a skintight, one-piece male workout leotard, with high-cut thong and banana hammock. *(Stupid Idea: Confuse and Perhaps Even Infuriate Your Customers.)*

Both were eventually revealed to be hoaxes, part of a series of silliness that the company perpetuates, particularly each April Fool's Day, but they still managed to attract a disproportionate amount of attention to the already well-established media darlings. Perhaps that's just the point.

And perhaps none of my Stupid Ideas are really all that stupid.

Tactic 8: A Piece of The Puzzle

Like Tactic 3, this one is also closely related to Chapter 6's Theory three. The little thing that means a lot here is a piece of the puzzle rather than the puzzle itself; like Ryan Karpeles said in Chapter 6, "Trees First, Forest Second."

The only problem we face, however, is deciding which of the trees we should choose. That's what this tactic tries to facilitate. Its method is straightforward, rooted in scientific distillation, and two-pronged:

1. Deconstruct the problem/opportunity/challenge into small pieces.

2. Concentrate on the shiniest one.

In the deconstruction process, you may find that there's more than one shiny piece. You may find that there isn't a great difference between any of the shiny pieces. (Worse yet, you may find that there's none at all, which may mean this Tactic is not for you.) Like in any Surprise marketing tactic though, it all comes down to a judgment call. Whether good or poor judgment prevails . . . well, we'll all find out in the end, won't we?

I'm still waiting to find out from Jeff Gruia. Jeff is the head of Seeqa International, an eyewear manufacturer that specializes in upscale fashion reading glasses and reader frames. One day last year, from out of the blue, he called me (perhaps knowledgeable of my obsession with sunglasses) and asked for help with this problem.

"I watch shows like *CSI* and *Law & Order* all the time, and I always see my competitors' frames on their characters," Jeff complained. "Is there a way I can get my glasses onto the people on these shows?"

"Sure," I said. "I can turn you onto a product placement consultant. They'll charge you about $100,000 and ask for an equivalent amount in product samples. Let's say they do their job really well—your frames and glasses will be seen all over the primetime players you covet.

"However, you'll still be faced with the real problem," I continued. "Nobody would know that they're yours. In fact, if you started this call by telling me that the glasses I see on these shows right now are yours, I'd probably believe you. I wouldn't know the difference."

Despite their color and unique designs, Seeqa glasses are rather undistinguishable from the competition. And at $100 or so a pair, they are in the high-end of nonprescription readers, thus an easy mark for cannibalization by lower-priced, discount-store copycats. The problem wasn't getting them on the TV screen; the problem was getting them on the radar screen.

So as a public service to a really nice guy, we spent some time "deconstructing" his true problem. We looked at price, sourcing issues, lens power, fit, packaging, placement at the retail level (they've cracked some major names, like Neiman-Marcus and Saks), before finally being blinded by the shiny object: why people wear them.

"Obviously, reading glasses are worn to read, but to read what?" I asked Jeff.

At first, he didn't get it, but then we started to list what people read with his—or any—glasses: summer "beach novels," financial statements, music, love letters, blogs, Black-Berries or cellphones, and books on Surprise marketing. We realized that "what" instead of "why" was the piece of the puzzle to concentrate on. Instead of just being another pur-veyor of "fashion eyewear," Seeqa could develop a line of "Lifestyle Eyewear." I'm sure you're already picturing the dif-ferent frames that could make "Business Glasses" or "Love Lenses" or "Mobile Eyes" stand out in the marketplace, and give rise to new designs in each category every year. Then all Jeff would have to do is wait as the folks from Jerry Bruck-heimer Productions and Dick Wolf Productions, producers of *CSI* and *Law & Order,* respectively, call him for glasses for their shows.

From glasses we move on to cups; coffee cups to be more specific. Following my speech at the Hotel Marketing and Sales conference I mentioned earlier in this book, I was con-fronted by a woman who owned a small resort hotel and was looking to do something special for her guests. She asked me what I thought of her idea of serving free coffee in the lobby.

I was polite, but bluntly honest.

"Look, nobody's going to complain, but frankly, lobby cof-fee's been done 1,000 times over," I told her. "What's your real objective?"

She told me that she wanted to show that although not part of a major chain, her hotel could do something special and be remembered for it à la Doubletree's ubiquitous cookie giveaway. Although I had a flight to catch, we spent a few min-utes deconstructing her challenge. We focused on the quality of the coffee given, the opportunity to gift each customer with a branded mug to take home, some snack to go with the coffee, but we weren't getting anywhere. We changed direction and considered who would staff this; would it be self-serve (a quick no) or handled by a staff member (although costlier, a better alternative to develop client interaction). We thought of staffing it with someone who sings (nixed because of the potential to become annoying), before moving the thought process to the actual location of the coffee cart.

And that's when the idea hit. As it stands now, hotel coffee can be served in three places: in rooms via room service, in on-site restaurants, and in the lobby. There's just one place remaining where someone would truly be Surprised to get a coffee—in the elevator. So the lobby coffee idea morphed into a petite coffee cart tucked into each elevator, served to the shocked with a smile from a real person every morning.

I didn't have much time, but as I left, we shook hands and the woman—whose name I never learned, by the way—made a vow that if she ever implements the elevator coffee cart idea, she would send me a picture of it in use to showcase on my blog—and maybe a steaming cup or two.

Tactic 9: Taking Things Out of Context

The genesis for this tactic occurred last winter when, while backing out of my garage to get to my weekly hockey game, I came upon a minor commotion. There, passed out in one of my neighbors' driveways, was a drunk man. His body was sprawled out like a Keith Haring character, making an obtuse snow angel in the fallen flakes, and over him hovered two of my 'hood's Good-est Samaritans, scratching their heads as to what to do with this unseemly and uninvited guest,

What does all this have to do with Surprise? Well, we all have, unfortunately, had to step over an inebriated body or two in our time. When they are in the vicinity of a city's downtown core, outside a club, or in some alley, they are disturbing, but accepted as part of the landscape. But when they are alone in a driveway of a well-to-do, residential suburb like the one I live in, far away from any bar or liquor store, they indeed ramp up the voltage on the Surprise meter. While I don't advocate drinking until you're facedown in the snow (particularly in the summer), the lesson here is that taking things out of their natural habitats and placing them where they are out of context helps drive what this book is all about.

The Out of Context tactic need not be a major ordeal— you can wear a baseball cap with a tux or running shoes with a suit; show up for a panel discussion at the Sports Marketing Conference in New York, direct from a one-hour run, wearing sweaty shorts and a skull cap (which I actually did a couple of years ago); play classical music in the dressing room before the big game (what my son's hockey team does, quite unexpected among 16- to 18-year-old boys with rampant testosterone), serve Coca-Cola in cham-pagne flutes ... anything that switches two norms into one "abnorm" is an easy Surprise recipe. Here are a number of examples from around the world for your cookbook:

This one always gets a huge reaction at my Surprise speeches. When you think of jewelry/fashion ads, you think of beautiful women staring off into the horizon with some sort of aloof, vacant gaze. Then there's this from Italy's Franco Pianegonda, the Richard Branson of jewelry, depicted in Figure 7.14.

This ain't no Cartier, or Van Cleef and Arpels; Pianegonda's battle cry is "Leave a Mark," and these bizarre ads are just part

Figure 7.14 Beauty is in the eye (and tongue) of the beholder.

of a marketing mix that includes a corporate philosophy guide that's tauntingly titled "Don't Read!" The ad itself is one of a series where gorgeous women and men make outrageous, out-of-character faces while modeling Pianegonda's pricey gold, silver, and diamond bling. In Milan, where you can suffer from designer overkill after a mere one-block stroll down Via Montenapoleone, Pianegonda's "on your face" attitude makes him a magnet for attention, and customers.

The concept of the Pop-Up continues to pop up. The "now you see it/now you don't" approach is classic Tactic 9. It goes like this:

1. *Where there once was nothing there is suddenly something.*

2. *This something is so different, it initiates buzz.*

3. *This buzz begets crowds.*

4. *Just before crowds tire of the concept, the something is taken away.*

5. *All that's left behind is perfect nothingness.*

Pop-Up has worked its magic in retail with trendy pioneers like Target, Nike, Method Home Cleaning Products, and mobile-only boutiques like New York's Caravan, taking to the streets (and in Target's case, to a ship). Now, trendsetters like Europe's Hotel Movil and Nikki Beach at Sea plan to bring the model to the hospitality sector. After that, what's next? Well, if a recent trip to Denmark is any indication, how about Pop-Up Hair Salons? Sounds nutty, but check out this picture (Figure 7.15).

Figure 7.15   A little off the top, a lot off the back.

I noticed this just off a busy Copenhagen street, and while trying to be discreet in taking the photo, the "stylist" called me over for a quick explanation (thankfully, as I thought he was going to confiscate my camera). Seems that he does a booming biz cutting the hair of the city's construction and road workers, and does in a few minutes what would take at least a half-hour in a shop, never mind the to-and-from travel time. Perhaps not for the tress-obsessed like me, but there is most definitely a clientele for this type of street service/theater, like the crowds at festivals, multiband outdoor rock events, pedestrian malls, street sales, and other such milieus of public spectacle. One man's haircut is another man's show.

Combining the luxury goods of Pianegonda and the Pop-Up theme comes the story of a concert I caught in Beaver Creek, Colorado, a resort town so "eleganza" it gives tony Vail urban street cred by comparison. I've been to thousands of rock concerts and have seen it all—or so I thought.

The show was by Dave Mason at The Vilar Center, Beaver Creek's intimate, wood-paneled concert hall. Box office is at street level, so to get to the floor seats one has to descend a grand staircase. Once there, to the immediate left of the center doors, was the perfunctory "Merch Table," resplendent with t-shirts, CDs, posters, and the like. Maximum price: $25. One color: black. That's it pictured in Figure 7.16.

But on the other side of doors was another souvenir vendor, one that gave new meaning to the term "Rock" Concert. There, behind two shining showcases, were rope-thick necklaces of emeralds, rubies, sapphires, and diamonds, multistrand tennis bracelets, higher-than-high-end watches, and gold earrings the size of walnuts. Many pieces were worth *way* more than the gross potential of the evening's entertainment (that's 530 seats at $55 each). That's it in Figure 7.17.

Figure 7.16 A rock concert . . .

Figure 7.17 . . . with $50,000 rocks.

Out-of-the-ordinary indeed, but easily rationalized I suppose, since Princess World Jewelers, the people behind the showcases, were also the people sponsoring the Vilar's winter season. Their presence was even easier rationalized given that the household income of most of the concert's attendees would dwarf the gross national product of many small nations.

By the way, guess which Merch Table had more traffic? Getting "stoned" at a concert never cost this much before . . . but I suspect the high lasts a whole lot longer . . . kaching!

When it comes to wine, I don't know my Shiraz from my elbow. When presented with the perfunctory wine list I read it, in the words of comedian Bobby Slayton, "like Jews read the Torah, from right to left; I see what the prices are, and then what wine goes with it." So imagine my delight when, at the end of a very filling and tastebud-popping meal at Emeril's in Atlanta, I was presented with something called "The Coffee List."

Featuring beans from Cafés Richard, France's leading coffee roaster, who have been brewing since 1875, the list includes everything from a $6 deep-roasted Italian Florio to a whopping $12 shot of Jamaican Blue Mountain, my favorite coffee in the world. This ain't the "load up with cream and sugar" stuff of coffee shops or resort hotel elevators; this is sniff tenderly and sip slowly liquid platinummmmm.

By raising the profile of this taken for granted after-dinner staple way above the Starbucks bar, Emeril's is not just adding big-time to its bottom line (do you know what the margin is on a 12-buck espresso shot?), but is giving me something to be geeky and overeducated about at a dinner table . . . a position that's truly out of context!

While on the subject of food, here are three more archetypal instances of Tactic 9 in play.

To kick off Bar-B-Q season, a promotional campaign for Bud Light in Canada offered two free sirloin steaks in specially-marked cases of 24 beers. While raising eyebrows and conjuring up some fairly unsavory mental images, the brewery indeed lived up to its promise, albeit without the unsanitary mess—it enclosed gift certificates from promo partner M&M Meat Shops.

Ingredient/nutrition lists are commonplace, mandatory even, on all packaged food. But on shoes? Yes, if you're the Timberland company. Timberland has borrowed the nutrition list concept for its products, starting with footwear, which outlines the environmental impact per unit manufactured with such measuring sticks as "Energy to Produce," "Global Warming Contribution," and "Material Efficiency." This makes the throwaway—sorry, the "recyclable"—shoebox a must-read.

And other than a roast beef banquet for vegetarians, nothing can be more out of context than what's for supper in Figure 7.18.

While some said it was a hoax or the work of PhotoShop, this was an actual sale item at Balducci's, a high-end Northeastern grocery chain. Attention, it got plenty of. But sales? The Jewish religion forbids the eating of any meat from the pig, and I don't think there was, or will ever be, an exception made for its annual Festival of Lights.

Sometimes, just a small position shift results in massive out-of-contextness. Many in the marketing world questioned the decision of State Farm Insurance buying TV ads on preschool haven Nickelodeon, but as the company rationalized, "It's crucial to reach consumers where they are."

Figure 7.18 Oy Vey...

And State Farm's adult clientele is watching the kiddie network . . . with their kids.

In Milan, the renowned art bookstore Libreria Bocca draws customers by the placement of its original works for sale—in the floor. A sheet of industrial-strength plexiglass has been laid over countless "tiles" of 15-by-15 inch paintings and photographs, which themselves have been the subject of two major exhibitions and many books. The floor is a cool and obvious conversation point, and one borne not just for aesthetics' sake, but for survival's. All of these works are donated by some of Italy's most notable contemporary artists, can be purchased for 500 Euros, with all proceeds going to help the store maintain its increasingly incongruent, hard-to-hold-onto spot among high-rent neighbors like Prada, Gucci, and Louis Vuitton in the 130-year-old Galleria Vittorio Emanuelle II.

Finally, to bring an end to Tactic 9 and this Ironman Marathon of a chapter, I bring you a startling ad from The UPS Store (Figure 7.19).

Figure 7.19

Yes, it was printed upside down. While following the conventional wisdom of being out of context, most ads like these usually disappoint; they're most often dopey, irrelevant gimmicks, like those college handbills that screamed "SEX!" and then let you down by saying "Now That I Have Your Attention . . ." But not this one. The photo of a despondent, head-in-hands sales guy was bolstered by the headline:

Think this upside-down page is surprising?
Imagine finding one in your presentation.

Brilliant use of awkward positioning and that sick feeling in the pit of our stomachs that we've all had to deal with at one time or another.

No such feeling now, though. After sifting through the theories and plowing through the tactics, you should be chomping at the bit to try your hand at Surprise marketing itself. Our final chapter will show you just how far and wide you can actually apply it.

Summary

CHAPTER 7 IS NOT OVER YET: REMEMBER TO

- Open your eyes again for the first time by wearing Virgin Contact Lenses.

- Mix speed and strength for optimal Shock and Ahh. . . .

- Emote! Words are important! Use them with flair!

- Find your inner stereotype and rebel against it.

- U-turn your head and check out the view in the rearview mirror.

- Nimbly plant today's Time Bombs for tomorrow's explosions of Pow!

- A seemingly stupid act may lead to a very smart result.

- Never mind the forest, concentrate on the trees.

- Displace people and things from their normal settings to out of context shock.

CHAPTER 8

The Tomorrow of Surprise

Enjoy them while they're here. The days of innocence may soon be over for Surprise.

A wonderful emotional paradox, we've seen that Surprise combines the unspoiled innocence of a child with the persuasive potency of the world's most hard-assed sales team; picture a Day Care Center run by the guys of Glengarry Glen Ross. The end result is a potent phenomenon that emerges naturally and influences widely—which seems to make Surprise too valuable to be left to its own devices.

As is the case with other powerful, natural phenomena like childbirth, sunlight, and human intelligence, scientists are currently trying to replicate the element of Surprise in laboratories. Seemingly harmless start-up companies like "MyStrands," "Pandora," and "What to Rent" are developing predictive algorithms that will in-vitro Surprise and eventually minimize it, at least in the domains of "what music you'll want to hear" or "what movie you'll want to see."

These showbizzy fun and games are just the Trojan horse, however. Max Levchin's appropriately named company, Slide, entered Web 2.0 by producing seemingly harmless Facebook applications, but at the root of his ambition is the more ominous building of a "machine that knows more about you than you know about yourself." Gulp . . . calling George Orwell.

Why the big rush? Consider Google. The company is worth upwards of $150 billion for delivering search. Imagine the value, then, of the entity that can successfully "deliver find."

A *Fortune* magazine piece on the gold-rush mentality surrounding predictability said, "There is no go-to discovery engine—yet. Building a personalized discovery mechanism will mean tapping into all the manners of expression, categorization, and opinions that exist on the web today. It's no easy feat, but if a company can pull it off . . . well, such a tool could change not just marketing, but all of commerce."[1]

It's not as far away as you may think. Surprise's version of Dolly the Sheep could be lurking in a Microsoft lab as you read this. A report called "Modeling Surprise" in the MIT *Technology Review* last year revealed:

> *While existing computer models predict many things fairly accurately, surprises still crop up, and we probably can't eliminate them. But Eric Horvitz, head of the Adaptive Systems and Interaction group at Microsoft Research, thinks we can at least minimize them, using a technique he calls surprise modeling.*

Horvitz stresses that surprise modeling is not about building a technological crystal ball to predict what the stock market will do tomorrow, or what al-Qaeda might do next month. But, he says, "We think we can apply these methodologies to look at the kinds of things that have surprised us in the past and then model the kinds of things that may surprise us in the future."[2]

Microsoft's vision may be far-out, in both headspace and timeline (it wouldn't be the first time). But Horvitz and group have already used it to launch a real-world application: SmartPhlow, a traffic-forecasting service that offers congestion predictions for markets across the United States and England, ranging in future-gazing from a mere several minutes to a whopping five days in advance. The MIT report explained how SmartPhlow differs from the current GPS-based traffic helpers already on the market.

Most people in Seattle already know that such-and-such a highway is a bad idea in rush hour. And a machine that constantly tells you what you already know is just irritating. So Horvitz and his team added software that alerts users only to surprises— the times when the traffic develops a bottleneck that most people wouldn't expect, say, or when a chronic choke point becomes magically unclogged.[3]

With all this technology in place today (never mind what Moore's Law promises tomorrow), with all these incredibly gifted people chasing all these obscene amounts of cash, does Surprise really have a chance in a world where everything will be predicted, expected, and seemingly predestined? Or will our lives be like a lunch conversation between two uber-wired netizens who, after reading each others' blogs, following each others' Twitter tweets, and listening to each others' Podcasts, have nothing left to say to each other except "I know. Yeah, I know"?

A doomsday scenario, perhaps, but not totally implausible. Commercial science may one day replicate intelligence, and be able to accurately forecast what we will buy. But unless our hearts and souls are replaced with silicon chips and wiring, nobody will be able to foretell how we will feel . . . and subsequently act. Even if, by some unprecedented act of God or the Devil, science finds a way to predict our actions, the rebellious spirit of human nature will take over and act contrarian to jam the forced Surprise. Watch for a regression to schoolyard stubbornness and Ayn Rand-ian free will; "if the machine says I will do this, then dammit, I will do that instead!"

This defiance reflects a reality that celebrated actor F. Murray Abraham said many moons ago: "The difficulty is capturing Surprise on film." In other words, it's hard to fake the deep emotion that permeates Surprise. Your face can register the shock, your body imitate that sudden jolt, but the true "feeling" of Surprise is difficult, if not impossible, to forcibly falsify.

So, if that hard rain really does fall, when the Big Brother of Business knows all and sells all, the future of Surprise may lie in noncommercial applications, namely social, charitable, environmental, and other "good for us all" causes. Surprise can reach into hearts and minds, not just wallets. Put another way, and putting a twist on futurist Ray Kurzweil, Surprise may be the machine of a new soul.

In many parts of the world, it's already started, like at Camp Okutta. The unique summer adventure camp for kids brewed up a cauldron of scandal when it made its debut. "Leave the hassle of registration to us," the camp's web site cheerfully offered. "We will collect your children when it suits us best. Openings come up when kids are injured or killed." Even more controversial were the camp's outdoorsy activities, which included grenade tossing, target practice using AK-47s, and a 24-hour live minefield, all demonstrated in online videos by kids in brightly colored Camp Okutta t-shirts. Then there was its infirmary policy, which stated: "Kids who complain of illness, homesickness, or fear are treated promptly. We force them to take amphetamines and a rudimentary mixture of cocaine and gunpowder."

After spending a few minutes on the site, it became obvious that Camp Okutta was a joke. But not a "funny ha-ha" joke; more like a "thank God it's just a joke" joke. The Camp was the method in which Dr. Samantha Nutt, founder and executive director of WarChild Canada and one of the planet's great do-gooders, chose to expose people to the real-life plight of children in countries like Darfur, Ethiopia, Ghana, northern Uganda, Sierra Leone, South Sudan, and Sri Lanka. Click on the site's "Where is Camp Okutta?" link and you're taken to WarChild.ca, which explains:

Camp Okutta does not exist. But camps like it exist all over the world. Every day children are trained for war, fight in war, and die in war. There are an estimated 250,000 children being used as soldiers right now. We would never stand for it here. So why are we letting it happen there?

Look closely—there may be a tear or two in the popped eyes of Surprise.

In another way, Austin Hill is also channeling the power of Surprise for a noble cause. A serial entrepreneur, his former company—Internet privacy service provider Zero-Knowledge Systems—was so controversial he was branded "an enemy of the state" and had to defend his web-surfing identity anonymity product in the *New York Times* and on *60 Minutes*. These days, Austin's world is much calmer, way more pleasant, almost utopian. His new, groundbreaking venture is called Akoha, a social reality game that exploits what he calls "the gift economy" to spread goodwill worldwide on a constantly Surprising basis.

Akoha starts with a collection of cards, each of which describes a good deed, like "Read 'n' Recycle: Give a book to a friend or stranger," "Take Me I'm Yours: Give one hour of your time to a friend or stranger," or "The Gift of Mystery: Give a Surprise gift to a friend or stranger." These cards are surreptitiously left to be found in public places to spread their instant karma later on (a classic Time-Bomb tactic!), or can be exchanged on a face-to-face basis for more immediate delightful shock. All acts of random niceness sparked by these cards are then recorded on the Akoha web site, where players earn both Karma and Kudos points; the former for carrying out each act, the latter as the Akoha community votes on what was done . . . in essence, rewarding you for your reward. The more points you amass, the better you do. And the better you do for others.

"I call it the 'Wikipedia of making the world a better place,'" Hill says. "For many people, life just happens to them; they're not in control. By performing Akoha deeds, people enjoy a feeling of empowerment and gratitude. Social science has shown that most people resist acts of kindness; they feel that something else is attached. We're trying to unload that baggage with this game, and spread positivity for the sake of positivity, and fun."[4]

The Akoha cards come in decks, which can be personalized with custom Surprise deeds for different companies, brands, personalities, or causes. So the next time someone hands you their card, look closely. It may not be for business.

Another social issue taken by Surprise is that of reckless driving. To shock the system and force drivers to reduce their speeds through a busy intersection in Cambridge, Massachusetts, city officials called on artist Wen-ti Tsen, who came up with a controversial 20-foot circular mural painted directly on the asphalt. The out-of-context-ness Surprised drivers into slowing down, if only to appreciate the work. "I know I slow down," said Lillian Hsu of the Cambridge Arts Council. "There's something in the road, so there's a moment of confusion and you slow down. Then you see it's flat and you drive over it."[5] (Sadly, the Philistine element of Cambridge seems to have won this battle; less than two years after its commission, after numerous vandalism attacks of splattered pink paint, Tsen's roundabout mural was paved over last summer. But throughout it all, people who drove through the artwork and ensuing mess did indeed reduce their speed, so . . .)

Taken one step further, flat plastic optical illusions of pyramid-shaped three-dimensional speed bumps were laid down in the middle of high-trafficked roads in Philadelphia and Phoenix. "At a mere $60 to $80 each, they cost a fraction of real speed bumps (which can run $1,000 to $1,500) and require little maintenance," said Richard Simon, deputy regional administrator for the U.S. Highway Safety Administration.[6]

But these innovative actions pale when compared to how the Danish Road Safety Council stopped speeding drivers in their tracks. With sheer audacity and the extreme devotion to the Shock and Ahh . . . tactic, these guys went over the top, kind of literally.

Their solution was a network of human signs, called the Speedbandits. Standing alongside Danish roads, the Speedbandits waved and shook large, round speed limit signs at offending drivers, urging, imploring, and sometimes taunting them to slow down. What made this personalized undertaking even more effective was that the Speedbandits were all young women, extremely attractive young women at that . . . and topless (ah, now you get the "over the top" reference).

In a "Spotlight on the World" Internet news report filled with uncensored, full-frontal shots, breathtaking Head Bandit Heidi Svendsen admitted: "Sure, what we do is extreme, but I know from my heart that what we are doing is working. People are slowing down, people are noticing."[7]

According to Julie Paulli Budtz, the person responsible for coming up with the Speedbandits idea, the outcome was that 33 percent of all 18- to 40-year-old Danish men were influenced to slow down by the Speedbandits. "The Danish Road Safety Council has had a long tradition using deterrence as a means to getting people to change attitudes towards speeding," she said, "but now time had come to try something new."

"Spotlight on the World" reporter Bart Sweeney revealed that sometimes the Speedbandits even worked too well, and showed scenes of Copenhagen gridlock as drivers came to a standstill, ogling and taking cell phone pictures of the bare-breasted sign wavers.

Incredible and impressive . . . now just imagine how much more effective the Speedbandits would be . . . if they were real. In a multidimensional thump of Pow!, the Speedbandits were a complete hoax, a Government-sponsored project existing only on the aforementioned "Spotlight" web video. Yet the concept was so strong, and the video so widely viral, that the real-life results for the Danish Road Safety Council were concrete. Paulli Budtz chuckles when she lists the Speedbandits viewing stats. "We made the movie thinking

'Never mind who it is from, but who it is for?'" she says. "It was originally seeded on 55 sites but has today spread to more than 6,760 sites and has been seen by more than 12 million people; over 3,000,000 in the States, 1,000,000 in Denmark and almost 500,000 in Canada. And 56 times in the Vatican State.

"Before making the movie we had a lot of discussions regarding the ethics," she continues. "However, both our Ministry of Justice and our Minister for Gender Equality said that it was okay that we made the movie as long as it had an effect."

It had such an effect that one German TV production company flew to Denmark, equipment in tow, looking to replicate the report for its homeland audience. Imagine their Surprise to learn that they themselves were the only boobs they would encounter on this trip.

Wherever, however, and whenever it is applied, the cause of Surprise is critical. But it pales in importance to its ultimate effect, particularly when used to trigger a change of social behavior, or a change of heart, a sentiment sublimely captured by *Time* magazine's Nancy Gibbs, who wrote:

> *Surprises, by their nature, come in disguise, masked sometimes as disappointments or detours, when they're in fact dreams turning solid, if you'll just step aside and give them some air.*[8]

So power up the jet stream, and solidify some dreams.

The dreams of others.

But especially the dreams of you.

Maybe this was what Ralph Waldo Emerson meant in the epic poem "Merlin I" when he urged us to "Mount to paradise/By the stairway of Surprise."

Your first step awaits.

Summary

CHAPTER 8: DON'T LET THAT INNOCENT LOOK FOOL YOU!

- Keeping Surprise surprising may soon be an arduous task, given science's and business's obsession with predictability.

- If Surprise can be modeled, then the model can be broken.

- Consider consolidating the power of Surprise for social and charitable work.

- Know that Surprise is equally effective on the heart and soul as it is on the wallet.

- Silliness and irreverence can have an exponentially positive effect on "social" Surprise.

A Diploma in Surprise

Though they came from all walks of life, from all parts of town, from different backgrounds, and varying income levels, just about everybody seated in Oscar Peterson Hall agreed on something: the proceedings had already gone on a little too long. Welcome to the St. George's High School annual graduation ceremonies.

Exactly 69 boys and girls dressed as men and women were about to close one chapter of their lives, and open the next. By now, the multiple valedictorian speeches had all been delivered. The fiftieth anniversary video had been played. Two different students, one on piano, the other on guitar, had demonstrated their musical prowess. The sole remaining item on the lengthy program was the official seal to mark the end of five years of learning—the seemingly endless distribution of diplomas.

Parents and siblings smiled but squirmed in their seats as school Principal Jim Officer, Head of Academics Scott Armstrong, and Head of Students Michel Lafrance stepped up to the mic in front of a ceremonially draped table, on which were piled exactly 69 high school diplomas. The mathematically inclined in the crowd did some internal ciphering and figured out that even at a mere 30 seconds per graduate—the calling of their name, the walk to the table, the congratulatory handshake, the brief exchange of *bons mots*—that they were in for at least another half-hour of tedium. "The things we do for our kids," went the collective silent mental sigh.

Mr. Officer opened and read the first diploma.

"Erin Wiltzer."

The pretty blonde girl got up from her front row seat, had her moment with the school's brass, and sat down. As she did, Mr. Officer called the next name.

"Yen-Tung Lin."

And so it went; a progression of progeny and potential, one after another.

"Joshua Adams."

"Bryan Zimmerman."

"Bianca Cordileone."

By now, even the most comatose parent took notice of the unconventional manner in which the diplomas were being handed out. A progressive school, St. George's had decided to do away with the tyranny of the alphabet and its order. Why should both Vishesh Abeyratne and Ariel Zuckerman be the ones routinely forced to wait an eternity at the opposite ends of the scholastic spectrum just because of their family names? The unsystematic distribution was a gallant undertaking, but to the observant, there was more going on than just a random roll call.

"Ellis Green."

"Meaghan Shevell."

"Jonathon Neil Greenberg."

Now at the halfway point, the students started to turn a little edgy and boisterous. One of them, the elfin Jacob Carsley-Mann, grimaced and threw down his arms in mock disgust when the speakers boomed his name.

This is high school graduation, Pow!-style. In an ingenious move instilled not only to maintain decorum but to intensify interest, St. George's had transformed its grad ceremony into a suspenseful game; *Survivor* without the exotic island, *American Idol* without the singing. Every graduating student had contributed two dollars into a pot. The last one called would take home the loot . . . and be showered with the resounding cheers of his or her peers.

"Hayes Nulman." (Well, there goes the chance that the school will actually pay me back something.)

"Kira Kott."

"Samia Hossian."

The St. George's faculty, an alternative bunch of creative types and free spirits, were now also starting to get rowdy. They had their own game going, purportedly with higher stakes. The right student at the finish line could mean dinner for two with wine for some educator and his or her significant other.

"Katie Schwarz."

"Eric Richard Greenberg."

"Rachel Shiner."

A look at the table showed that the candidates had thinned to a handful. The tension in the room was palpable. You could cut it with a mortarboard.

"Jacob Lavigne."

"Lara Sancton."

With the end in sight, the "Awwws!" and the good-natured moans of disappointment were increasingly audible, as gravy trains ran off the rails and meal tickets went down the garburator.

"Andrew Sherman."

"Ariel Charney."

The room went silent as Scott Armstrong held the last two diplomas aloft. In a "push me/pull you"-like shuffle, he and Jim Officer jokingly tussled over the final pair, before choosing what was going to be the runner up. Upon hearing Mr. Officer utter just the first syllable of the name, the student body erupted en masse:

"Tiffy-B! Tiffy-B! Tiffy-B!"

Forget the name that was just called. The 2008 St. George's last grad standing was Tiffany Michelle Brasgold, who collected her most notable diploma, and the reward that went with it, with a Kleigl-light beam.

The real lesson learned at this academic exercise: the euphoric shock of Surprise can work everywhere. Surprise brightens lives, enhances stories, and renders the most stultifying event exciting, intriguing, entertaining, and fun. Surprise is like Hamburger Helper for life. It takes what you've come to know and love, tosses in a bit of spice, and renders it something new, fresh, and word-worthy.

Surprise inspires new ways of thinking, new ways of acting, and most importantly, new ways of interacting.

The only excuse for it *not* working is the one you will make.

For people, when faced with the decision to. . .

OKAY, WE'RE DONE HERE.
Sorry for the abrupt interruption, but I think by now you get the point.
For a real Surprise, turn the page...

The End of Pow!

Guess what? You're in.

Selected first edition copies of *Pow! Right Between the Eyes* have been chosen and reprinted to provide a special Surprise ending. Congratulations, because yours is one of them.

As part of this privileged, exclusive group, you are invited to call the following phone number at any time to formally culminate your relationship with this book: **1-866-POW-5677**

The call will give you additional insight, and provide the missing pieces necessary to fully optimize your experience and bring it to a satisfying close. Frankly, without it, the book is woefully incomplete.

And what about the others not lucky enough to get their hands on a special copy of *Pow!*? What can we say? It's unfortunate, but that's the luck of the draw. Too bad. Please don't tell them about this.

Thanks for reading *Pow! Right Between the Eyes*, and enjoy its unforegone conclusion!

AFTERWORD BY DAVID ALLEN
Science of Surprise? Who Knew?

David Allen is the author of Getting Things Done: The Art of Stress-Free Productivity, Ready for Anything: 52 Productivity Principles for Work, *and* Life Making It All Work: Winning at the Game of Work and Business of Life.

In the course of my professional life I became recognized as an expert in the arena of personal and organizational productivity—hardly a field one would associate with the positive power of surprise. "Personal effectiveness" is more often coupled with structure and control than deliberate unexpectedness. But in an interesting way my attraction to serendipity and spontaneity as a way of being is what led me down a path exploring the discipline of focus and systems. I love freedom—especially of the emotional and mental sort—and many of the best practices of productivity alleviate the distractions and pressures that can easily diminish the ability to have that kind of fun.

It wasn't until I read this book that I realized the relationship between my lifelong love of humor and my fascination with much of the Zen aesthetic. Both can assist us in breaking the bounds of our conditioned and inflexible thinking and beliefs. Both can increase the space we can give to the love of life. Both have surprise at their core.

And who knew that there was a veritable science of surprise, as well as an art?! Kudos to Andy Nulman for demystifying such a universally valuable component of the human experience and providing practical tips and techniques for getting more of it.

Notes

Prologue

1. EDMUNS Inside Line (Edmunds.com), June 27, 2005.

Chapter 1

1. ThinkExist.com.
2. Laura M. Holson, "Caught on Film: A Growing Unease in Hollywood," *New York Times*, August 19, 2006.
3. *Windsor Star*, November 11, 2006.
4. Seth Godin blog, February 24, 2007.
5. Rafat Ali, PaidContent.org, May 23, 2007.
6. "Keeping It Cool," *Fast Company*, March, 2008, 32.
7. Danielle Sacks, "Crème de la Curator," *Fast Company*, May, 2008, 57.
8. Mike Beirne, "Q&A: Declaring 'War Against Beige,' IHG Personalizes," *Brandweek*, http://www.brandweek.com/bw/news/spotlight/article_display.jsp?vnu_content_id=1003546272.
9. Patti Summerfield, "Pass It On," *Strategy Magazine*, 28.
10. Jack Neff, "Consumers Rebel Against Marketers Endless Surveys," *Advertising Age*, https://listserve.temple.edu/cgi-bin/wa?A2=ind0610a&L=mmc&P=3074.
11. Barbara Kiviat, "Word on the Street," *Time*, 40.
12. "I Sold it Through the Grapevine," *BusinessWeek*, http://www.businessweek.com/magazine/content/06_22/b398606.htm.
13. Andy Sernovitz, *Word of Mouth Marketing: How Smart Companies Get People Talking* (Kaplan Business: New York, NY), 9–10.

14. James Surowiecki, "The Decline of Brands," *Wired*, http://www.wired.com/wired/archive/12.11/brands.html.

15. John Gaudiosi, "Playing With Numbers," *Marketing* Magazine, April 28, 2008, 12.

16. BrainyQuote.com.

17. Watts Wacker and Ryan Mathews, *The Deviant's Advantage: How Fringe Ideas Create Mass Markets* (Crown Business: New York, NY), 151.

18. Jeff Jensen, "Spoiler Nation: Secrets About Movie/TV Secrets Revealed!," June, 2008, http://www.ew.com/ew/article/0,,20203864,00.html.

19. Elizabeth Renzetti, "I Felt Like Screaming Every Time A New Song Started," April 26, 2008, C1.

20. Jeffrey M. O'Brien, "Wii Will Rock You," *Fortune*, 86.

21. Lev Grossman, "A Game For All Ages," *Time*, May 15, 2006, 29.

22. "Wii Will Rock You," *Fortune*, 86.

23. "How Apple Got Everything Right By Doing Everything Wrong," March, 2008, http://www.wired.com/techbiz/it/magazine/16-04/bz_apple.

24. A.G. Lafley and Ram Charan, "The Consumer is Boss," *Fortune*, March 17, 2008, 122.

25. Jordan Ellenberg, "This Psychologist May Outsmart the Math Brains Competing for the Netflix Prize," *Wired*, March, 2008, 118.

26. Ibid., 116.

Chapter 2

1. David Ogilvy, "Ogilvy on Advertising," 167.

2. Professors Pierre, Baldi, Laurent Itti and Douglas Muñoz, http://ilab.usc.edu/surprise/.

3. Ibid.

4. Nassim Nicholas Taleb, *The Black Swan: The Impact of the Highly Improbable* (Random House: New York, NY), xxvii.

5. Chip Heath and Dan Heath, *Made To Stick: Why Some Ideas Survive and Others Die* (Random House, New York, NY), 68.

6. Ibid., 67.

7. "CPU: A Unit of Measurement for Both Creatives and Marketers," http://goliath.ecnext.com/coms2/gi_0199-7924592/CPU-a-unit-of-measurement.html.

8. Jessi Hempel and Michael V. Copeland, "Are His Widgets Worth Half A Billion?," *Fortune*, March 31, 2008, 38.

9. "The Long Tail Author's New Idea Is Free!," *Brandweek*, March 24, 2008, 5.

10. "Post Modernism Is the New Black," December 19, 2006, http://www.financialexpress.com/old/print.php?content_id=150052.

11. www.Kia.com.

12. Jennifer Reingold, "Target's Inner Circle," March 31, 2008, 80.

13. Steven Leckar, "15th Anniversary: The Brian Eno Evolution," *Wired*, http://www.wired.com/techbiz/media/magazine/16-06/st_15th_eno.

14. Chip Heath and Dan Heath, *Made To Stick: Why Some Ideas Survive and Others Die* (Random House, New York, NY), 71.

Chapter 3

1. Jonathan Rausch, "Sex, Lies, and Videogames," November, 2006, http://www.theatlantic.com/doc/200611/rauch-videogames.

2. Tom Peters, *The Pursuit of Wow!: Every Person's Guide to Topsy-Turvy Times* (Vintage: New York, NY), 103.

3. http://discussionleader.hbsp.com/taylor/2008/05/wy_zappos_pays_new_employees_t.html.

4. "Reinvent Yourself. Repeat," December, 2005, 124.

5. "Cards Go 2.0," June, 2007, http://money.cnn.com/magazines/business2/business2_archive/2007/06/01/100050973/index.htm?postversion=2007061916.

6. Stuart Elliott, "A Majority of One," *New York Times*, February 27, 2007, http://query.nytimes.com/gst/fullpage.html?res=9402EFD81038F936A25754C0A9679C8B63.

7. Ibid.

8. http://www.swlearning.com/marketing/mktg/mktg_1e/themktgstory.html.

9. David Hochman, "When Chekhov Meets Whoopee Cushion," February 27, 2005, http://www.swlearning.com/marketing/mktg/mktg_1e/themktgstory.html.

10. www.newmuseum.org.

Chapter 4

1. Jennifer Lee, *The Fortune Cookie Chronicles* (Twelve), 3.

2. "Why We're So Obsessed With 'Next,' " September 8, 2003, 71.

3. "Why Costco Is So Damn Addictive," 126.

4. "Friends in High Places," *Marketing* magazine, February 25, 2008, 30.

5. www.gamespot.com.

6. Douglas Rushkoff, *Get Back in the Box* (Collins Business: New York, NY), 129–30.

7. Daniel Gilbert, *Stumbling Upon Happiness* (Vintage: New York, NY), 130.

8. David Mamet, *The Wicked Son* (Schocken: Germany), 61.

Chapter 5

1. "The Unthinkable ... And The Mundane," *Fast Company*, September, 2004, 83.

2. Peter Georgescu, "Creativity to the Rescue," *Fortune*, October 15, 2007, 74.

3. Robert Shelton, *No Direction Home: The Life and Music of Bob Dylan* (Da Capo Press: New York, NY), 438.

4. Becky Ebenkamp, "Chipping Away at Frito with 'Stem Cell' Snacks," *Brandweek*, January 7, 2008, 13.

5. Linda Tischler, "Stark Raving," *Fast Company*, October, 2007, 125.

6. http://tv.winelibrary.com.

Chapter 6

1. Tim Purtell, "Billy Wilder Speaks," *Entertainment Weekly*, October 20, 2006, 65.

2. Linda Tischler, "The Beauty of Simplicity," *Fast Company*, November, 2005, 56.

3. http://ryankarpeles.blogspot.com/2007/picture-this.html.

4. Personal phone interview with Sami Bay of Something-Store.com.

5. Ibid.

Chapter 7

1. Denise Shekerjian, *Uncommon Genius* (Peguin: New York, NY), 33.

2. http://www.socaltech.com/Insights/showarticle.php?id= 00033.

3. "5 Rules of Guerrilla Marketing," Constantine Von Hoffman, November 20, 2006, 29.

4. Melanie Warner, "Snacks Go On a Diet: U.S. Food Makers Downsize Portions," May 30, 2005, http://www.iht.com/articles/2005/05/29/business/portion.php.

5. Ibid.

6. Jeremy Caplan, "Hold the Ice Cream!," *Time*, Special Global Business Section, August, 2005, http://www.time.com/time/magazine/article/0,9171,1083937,00.html?iid=digg_share.

7. http://www.stmarystoday.com/News/FreeCoffintoFirstDWI DeadDriver.html.

8. Corey Hajim, "The Weird Al of Wall Street," *Fortune*, June 11, 2007, 25.

9. Richard Morgan, "Reverse Graffiti," *New York Times*, December 10, 2006, 68.

10. Helen Carter, "Graffiti Artist's New Form of Street Art Under Fire," *The Guardian*, October 15, 2004, http://www.guardian .co.uk/uk/2004/oct/15/ukcrime.prisonsandprobation.

11. Matthew Grimm, "A Whole New Hind of Media," *Brandweek*, July 12, 2004, 26.

12. TheFunniest.com.

13. David Kushner, "Rebel Alliance: How a Small Band of Sci-Fi Geeks Is Leading Hollywood Into a New Era," *Fast Company*, May, 2008, 100.

Chapter 8

1. Jeffrey M. O'Brien, "You're Sooooooooo Predictable," November 27, 2006, 228.

2. M. Mitchell Waldrop, "Modeling Surprise," March/April, 2008.

3. Ibid.

4. Personal interview with Austin Hill.

5. John Glassie, "Speed Reducing Art," *New York Times*, December 10, 2006.

6. http://www.azcentral.com/news/articles/2008/06/27/ 20080627fakespeedbumps0627.html.

7. Personal interview and email correspondence with Julie Paulli Butz.

8. Nancy Gibbs, "Graduates, Go Forth and Multiply!," *Time*, June 16, 2008, 48.

About the Author

Andy Nulman's only regret is that he has just one life to live . . . but he's working on a solution. While young in spirit, he's a hardened business vet with over 30 years of diverse experience that has seen him launch Just For Laughs, the world's largest comedy event, produce more than 150 TV shows all over the globe, cofound the groundbreaking mobile entertainment pioneer and cofound the groundbreaking mobile entertainment pioneer Airborne Mobile, which he sold for over $100 million, bought back for way less, and where he continues to work today with brands like *Maxim*, *Family Guy*, and The NFL. In his spare time, Andy is an acclaimed and dynamic public speaker/showman, half-decent snowboarder, hot-and-cold hockey goalie, limited-ranged rock singer, and adventurous stage director. Married with two grown children and two rambunctious dogs, he never, ever fails to Surprise.

Reach out!
Email: andy@andynulman.com
Blog: www.powrightbetweentheeyes.com
Twitter: @andynulman

Index